SCHOLASTIC

YOU CAN

Teach your class to LISTEN

Sue Palmer

FOR AGES 4-7

"Listening must be planned for, taught, veloped and assessed"

DfES

Acknowledgements

Author
Sue Palmer

Editor
Kathleen McCully

Development Editor
Kate Pedlar

Series Designer
Joy Monkhouse

Cover Designer
Anna Oliwa

Cover Illustration
© Corbis/PunchStock

Design and Illustrations
Q2a Media

Designed using Adobe InDesign

Published by Scholastic Ltd
Villiers House
Clarendon Avenue
Leamington Spa
Warwickshire CV32 5PR

www.scholastic.co.uk

Printed by Bell and Bain Ltd.
1 2 3 4 5 6 7 8 9   7 8 9 0 1 2 3 4 5 6

You Can Teach Your Class to Listen is based on the author's research for a previous book – *Toxic Childhood: How the Modern World is Damaging our Children … and What We Can Do About it* (Sue Palmer © 2006 Orion) – in which she brought together the work of a range of academics concerned with child development and language and listening skills acquisition. This included neuroscientists, Early Years specialists, developmental psychologists, linguistics experts and speech and language therapists.

The teaching ideas in *You Can Teach Your Class to Listen,* are the result of five years of meetings with Early Years teachers, around the UK. This book is therefore dedicated to all those teachers, who shared their practice so generously. S.P

British Library Cataloguing-in-Publication Data
A catalogue record for this book is available from the British Library.
ISBN 978-0439-94532-5

Contents

Contents

Introduction

In terms of learning, listening is probably the most important skill of all. If children can't listen effectively, they have trouble acquiring language and learning to read. And they find it difficult to pay attention in class, which means they're likely to struggle with learning across the curriculum.

Sadly, more and more children now have problems with listening. One of the unintended side effects of modern life has been the impact it has had on children's language and listening skills. In disadvantaged areas of the country, schools now expect language delay in 50 per cent or more of their Reception intake. And language delay is closely associated with – and is usually a result of – listening problems. If children can't listen naturally, then we have to teach them. Yet, most teachers have never had any training in how to improve children's listening skills. This book has been written to fill that gap.

What are listening skills... and how do I teach them?

Chapter 1 defines the skills that make a good listener. If you grew up in the days when listening developed naturally, you probably aren't aware of how good you are at listening, and why. Your understanding of the elements involved is probably implicit rather than explicit. But once you *are* aware of the key skills, you can target them specifically in all class activities.

Chapter 2 helps you to listen more effectively yourself, and to model good listening skills for the children. Your example is critical to developing the skills of your class.

Chapters 3 to 6 suggest a range of opportunities for developing specific skills through a variety of teaching and learning activities appropriate for four- to seven-year-old children. Most activities involve the use of listening skills to help fulfil other curricular objectives. On the whole, listening is not an 'add-on', to be tackled in a series of one-off lessons. It has to underpin everything you do in the classroom, across the full range of the curriculum.

Chapter 7 therefore continues this theme of listening throughout the school day, by looking at generic organisational and teaching methods.

But these suggestions are only starting points. Once you are aware of what good listening involves, you can look for other ways of targeting the key skills to ensure their steady, incremental development in all your pupils. This is the real joy and professionalism of teaching – not simply following the suggestions in a book, but finding your own ways to adapt, improve and extend them – ways that work for you, with your particular children, in your particular school and circumstances. Have fun turning your class into good listeners!

You Can... Help children sit still

Before children can sit and listen, they need good physical coordination and control.

Thinking points

- The ability to be still depends on a mature vestibular system (our inner sense of body awareness and balance). Young children – particularly boys – need lots of running, jumping, clambering and climbing before they are ready for standing (or sitting) still.
- When you ask children to sit in a space, do some of them insist on leaning against furniture or each other? Children with a poorly developed sense of their body's position in space feel the need to make contact with a surface to help them balance. They're probably not trying to be 'naughty', just dealing with an immature vestibular system.
- For more information on how movement underpins behaviour, language and learning, see:
  - www.jabadao.org
  - *The Well-Balanced Child* by Sally Goddard Blythe (Hawthorn Press).

Tips, ideas and activities

- Don't expect children who are physically uncoordinated to listen and attend well. Concentrate on the basic skills of coordination, body awareness and balance before expecting attentiveness.

- Provide plenty of opportunities for children to move about freely, especially outdoors. Boys particularly need to learn control of big movements – through active, imaginative outdoor play – before they can develop small-scale coordination and control.

- Moving to music is a great way to develop control (see pages 30–31). Patterned rhythmic music helps children pattern their body movement, and moving to music with others helps develop social skills. Let children:
  - move freely to the music, choosing their own movements
  - copy simple sequences of movements that you show them.

- Be sure to provide plenty of activities involving cross-lateral movement (moving alternate sides of the body, which helps the two sides of the brain work in harmony), for example:
  - marching to good marching tunes
  - games that involve crawling
  - climbing up climbing frames or ladders.

- Keep an eye on children with attention problems when they are playing or doing PE. What sort of coordination tasks do they have trouble with? How can you devise activities that will help them improve their physical control?

You Can... Help children discriminate sounds

Listening, speaking and, eventually, literacy all depend on children's ability to discriminate between language sounds. Many children – especially boys – need to spend time developing these skills before they can make progress at school.

Thinking points

- The ability to discriminate foreground sounds used to develop naturally through a baby's early interaction with its mother (or carer). In a noisy multimedia world, this can no longer be taken for granted. Electronic communication now distracts adults from talking and singing to little babies and distracts babies and toddlers from attending to adults.
- Research in inner city areas in the late 1990s showed nearly 50 per cent of one-year-olds were behind schedule in discriminating foreground sounds against background noise.
- Spoken language (and later, literacy) depends on children being able to discriminate the 44 phonemes of English (photocopiable page 56). They can only learn to do this if they have plenty of 'data' to work on. That data comes from being in an environment rich in language, songs and rhymes, and plenty of individual attention.

Tips, ideas and activities

- Teach children the most basic listening skill of all – discriminating a foreground sound against background noise – through playing 'Dodgems':
  - You need a whistle or anything that makes a distinctive noise.
  - Tell the children they are going to be dodgem cars rushing around making a noise, but not bumping into each other. When they hear the whistle, they must stop immediately.
  - Play the game until the children get the hang of it. Then repeat it at regular intervals, using different sounds for the signal (bell, tambourine, cymbal...).
  - Give children who have difficulty playing the game extra practice in smaller groups, with the opportunity for personal attention.

- The next stage is to help children to discriminate between a range of sounds. Go on regular 'Listening Walks' around the school and the school environment. Stop every so often and listen for, say, 15 seconds. How many sounds can the children hear and identify?

- Do lots of songs, rhymes and language play to help children discriminate the sounds of the English language (see page 34). Teach rhymes that emphasise each of the consonant phonemes (see photocopiable page 56), and listen individually to those children you are worried about to see if there are any they don't articulate.

- The sooner children learn to discriminate sounds, the easier it will be for them. So try to convince parents of the importance of spending time talking, listening, singing and rhyming with their very young children. It is best if this is done in English, but interaction in any language is much better than no interaction at all. You can find more information and useful 'tip sheets' for parents on the Talk To Your Baby website (www.talktoyourbaby.org.uk).

You Can... Teach social listening skills

*Social listening involves a number of social conventions, such as looking at the speaker, taking turns and **actively** listening to what the speaker has to say.*

Thinking points

- Many children today find eye contact difficult. In some cultures it is considered rude, so you will have to explain (to children and parents) that eye contact in school is both OK and necessary.

- A more frequent cause of poor eye contact is too much screen-based activity outside school. A recent British study found that a majority of six- to eight-year-olds were more interested in looking at a blank screen than a human face. Since facial expression is a key way of communicating emotion, this is a disturbing development.

Tips, ideas and activities

- If children find it difficult to make eye contact, provide activities that help them look at you and each other. Similarly, provide directed activities to develop turn-taking. You can use daily social interactions in the classroom for this (such as the 'greeting' activity on page 14), or you can explicitly practise skills in PSHE. Chapter 4 on circle time provides many suggestions.

- Social conventions are relatively easy to teach because they relate to outward behaviour. But the skill of active listening – focusing on what the speaker is saying, and trying to understand it – goes on inside your head. Talk about this with your better listeners in small groups. Usually they can describe what good listening looks like ('the listener sits still, the listener asks questions if something isn't clear'). But can anyone describe what active listening *feels* like? This sort of discussion raises children's awareness (and yours!) of what listening involves.

- Young children listen naturally when they are motivated – if they want to know what someone is saying, they will listen. So when children's interest is fired by some event in or around the classroom, follow it up. Always take advantage of children's interest – you will achieve much more that way than by following a careful plan that sends everyone to sleep.

- We then have to help children transfer the natural motivation (from events and activities that naturally inspire their interest) to the day-to-day stuff of school learning, which sometimes is not fundamentally interesting to small children. This is a long and delicate task – it can't be rushed.

- The first and most important teaching strategy is to model good listening yourself, which is why Chapter 2 is devoted to this topic.

You Can... Develop children's auditory memory

All learning relies on memory, and for school learning (especially literacy and numeracy skills), auditory memory is very important indeed. But children reared in a multimedia age need lots of help to develop this key skill.

Thinking points

- One of the most important learning mechanisms is *repetition*. The more children repeat something, the stronger the neural network established in the brain. Repeating a sequence of words, rhythm and actions (in an action song or rhyme) is particularly powerful.
- Copying words and actions modelled by you also draws on another hugely important human learning strategy: *imitation*.
- While auditory memory may be poor, children reared in a multimedia age tend to have good visual memory. With plenty of opportunities for movement and outdoor play, they will also develop kinaesthetic and spatial memory. That is why it is so important to link auditory memory to these other ways of remembering.

Tips, ideas and activities

- Children need to commit many things to memory during their school careers, for example:
  - personal details, such as name, address, phone number, date of birth
  - essential information, such as the days of the week, months of the year, alphabet, number bonds, times tables
  - useful mnemonics, such as 'Thirty days hath September', 'Richard Of York Gave Battle In Vain' (for the colours of the rainbow), and ways of remembering tricky spellings.

- Use these, as appropriate for your class, to help train their auditory memory. For instance, at the beginning of term, ask each child to learn the personal details listed above, to tell you in circle time. With younger children, you could do this one item at a time; with older ones, the whole collection (*'My name is... I live at... and* my *phone number is... I was born on...'*).

- When essential or useful information has to be committed to memory, use tricks like:
  - rhythmic chanting by the whole class (lots and lots of times)
  - singing it (there are plenty of alphabet and tables songs, but you can also make your own songs, by putting your own words to a simple familiar tune)
  - adding actions (for instance, when learning the spelling mnemonics 'w-hen' and 'w-hat', let children say them repeatedly while making hen-like pecking movements or miming the exaggerated putting on and taking off of a hat).

- Start improving their powers of auditory memory from the moment children arrive in your class by teaching them a new rhyme or song every week and using books and stories with which they can join in and gradually learn by heart. For more detail about these activities, see Chapters 6 and 7.

You Can... Develop children's imaging skills

If we want children to be creative and imaginative, we have to develop their powers of mental imagery. This is closely associated with listening skills.

Thinking points

- Most adults learned mental imagery through listening to stories, descriptions, poems or songs, and imagining what they looked like. But the availability of vivid images on TV, DVDs and websites, as well as beautifully-produced picture books, mean today's children don't have the same opportunities to develop this skill. Indeed, constant spoon-feeding with vivid images means many don't know that it is possible to make your own mental pictures.
- As well as the development of imagination for writing stories and so on, the ability to visualise pictures and symbols (and to orientate them in space) is important for:
  - understanding numbers and spatial arrangements
  - remembering, predicting, logical thinking.

Tips, ideas and activities

- Introduce children to the idea of 'making pictures in their heads' by asking them to stare at a blank space on the wall. Then ask them to 'Make your own picture' while you read a *very* short description or poem, such as Christina Rossetti's *Caterpillar* (see photocopiable page 57). Ask them to describe what they saw.

- Don't be put off if many of the children are bewildered. Usually there are several who genuinely expect an image to appear on the wall, as if someone had switched on a TV. Let these non-visualisers listen to the children who are able to imagine, and talk about the 'pictures in their heads'.

- Look out for ways to develop this skill through other listening activities across the curriculum, for example:
  - In maths, can children imagine two rabbits, three rabbits, etc (and clap/blink/tap on the table for each rabbit they can see in their heads)?
  - In PSHE, can children visualise a calm, quiet, special place that they can go to in their heads when things get too much for them (page 28)?
  - Can children visualise what they did yesterday? Can they organise memories in sequences in their heads?
  - Can children draw or paint pictures from out of their heads? Can they illustrate a story read or told without pictures? (All art activities provide opportunities to develop mental imagery.)

You Can... Build up children's listening stamina

Not only do we have to teach children to listen, we also have to teach them how to listen for increasingly long periods. This requires an incremental approach.

Thinking points

- Developing any skill requires thoughtful incremental teaching, with plenty of praise for achievement at each stage. You have to break down skills, concepts and knowledge into small, motivating chunks - teaching them slowly but surely, giving plenty of praise for success at each stage. The more difficult the subject-matter, the smaller the chunks have to be.
- Children brought up in a multimedia world are not used to attending for long. If they miss something on DVD or CD, they can just rewind and replay. If something is boring, it is just a question of fast-forwarding or changing channels. We have to use incremental teaching to help them to attend when it matters.
- Poor listening skills are often behind 'naughtiness'. As described on page 6, lack of bodily awareness and coordination can cause problems attending and lead to irritating behaviour. Emotional problems can also cause children to be inattentive. If you are aware of the difficulties children are facing, it becomes easier to work out how to break down your teaching to suit them.

Tips, ideas and activities

- Don't expect children to run before they can walk. All children – especially the very young – need gradual training to build up listening stamina. Gauge what is a reasonable length of time to expect the children in your class to concentrate on oral work, and give plenty of praise when they reach or exceed your expectations.

- Specifically target listening stamina during circle time and storytime (suggestions for activities are given in the relevant chapters), but remember its importance across the curriculum. For instance, whenever you introduce a new activity that involves listening, start with very short bursts. As children develop their skills, gradually extend the length of time you continue the activity. This applies both to small groups and the whole class.

- Listening is usually only one skill among many in the activities you use for teaching. Make new activities as easy as possible by being sure about:
    - exactly what you want to convey
    - what you require of the children
    - the fact that it is something they are likely to succeed at.

  Then be very clear (and brief) in introducing and explaining it.

- If necessary, reduce the challenge by reducing the size of the group. For instance, if some children have trouble playing listening games in the whole class, give them the chance to practise (and succeed) in a small group first. The confidence of succeeding in the small group situation should set them up for success in the larger group.

- Whenever you expect children's full attention, make sure they know by using a visual sign or symbol (see page 47).

You Can... Help children internalise new vocabulary

Children learn new words and ideas through listening – but many are quickly forgotten. You can help them internalise words by careful targeting.

Thinking points

- A child's *receptive* vocabulary refers to the words she/he recognises in context. It is usually much larger than *expressive* vocabulary, which is the words she/he actually uses. For words to move from their receptive vocabulary into their expressive vocabulary, children need:
  - thorough understanding of them
  - opportunities to use them in context.

If children only hear new words (as on TV), the word usually goes 'in one ear and out the other'.

- Researchers at London University have found that explicit teaching of vocabulary in the way described above also leads to all-round improvements in children's language.

Tips, ideas and activities

- When introducing a new theme or topic, make a list of the key vocabulary you want children to remember. If, for instance, you are doing a topic on animals, you might want to include words like *mammal, nocturnal* or *hibernate.*
  - Target one word at a time. Introduce it within a meaningful context, saying what it means and asking children to repeat it. (*A badger is a nocturnal animal. That means it sleeps in the day and comes out at night. Nocturnal. Can you say that with me? … nocturnal, nocturnal, nocturnal… very good. Who can say it for me? Can you remember what it means?*)
  - Give plenty of opportunities for children to repeat the word, and talk about it. (*Can you think of other animals that are nocturnal? Do you think people are ever nocturnal? What would it be like if children were nocturnal?*)

- Set up an activity in which children have an opportunity to use the word and concept within a meaningful context (for instance, sorting pictures of animals into 'nocturnal' and 'daytime' and sticking them on a black or light blue poster).

- It also helps if everyone working with the children is aware of key vocabulary that you want the children to internalise. A 'words of the week' poster can act as a reminder to you, the children, teaching assistants and parents.

You Can... Help children internalise language structures

Children learn the structures of language through a natural process: listen – imitate – innovate. It relies on auditory memory and a physical 'feel' for pattern and rhythm. This is why a language-rich environment is essential in the early years.

Thinking points

- All the attention on literacy teaching in recent years has overlooked the huge importance of listening. Written language patterns are very different from spoken language patterns, and if children have not listened to enough 'literate language' patterns they will not be able to imitate them, either in speech or writing.

Tips, ideas and activities

- When we start teaching literacy skills and want children to know what 'a sentence' is, it is no good relying on explanations. Instead, we have to aim from the very beginning of education to give them a 'feel' for what sentences are. So provide lots of opportunities for children to *listen* to sentences (using repetition to help them hear the echoes in their heads), and let them get used to the 'feel' of producing sentences from their own mouths, by *imitating* what they hear.

- Circle time is an ideal opportunity to use the *listen – imitate – innovate* technique because many circle time activities involve 'sentence frames' (see page 29). Storytime is also rich in opportunities as children listen to you 'read aloud' and then imitate by 'reading along' with you (see pages 39–40). Once a selection of written sentence structures is firmly embedded in children's heads, this will provide a basis on which children can *innovate* when they want to express ideas for themselves.

- The more we develop children's auditory memory through rhythm, rhyme, music and song (pages 35–36), the easier they will find it to internalise the rhythms and patterns of literate language.

- Teaching literacy is all about moving children from the simple, fragmented patterns of spoken language to the more structured, explicit, organised patterns of written language. To familiarise them with literate language patterns, we have to give them opportunities to *listen – imitate – innovate* on the sentence structures of writing.This relies on the basic principles of good teaching:
  - simple, incremental steps that build up competence very gradually
  - opportunities to imitate
  - lots and lots of enjoyable repetition
  - motivating activities, at the right level for the child
  - plenty of success, providingthe motivation to continue.

You Can... Model active listening

There is so much extraneous noise in our lives these days that we have all learned to switch off from much of it. Active listening is about consciously switching on, and staying switched on.

Thinking points

- Active listening is essential to 'sustained shared thinking', which research has shown to be hugely important for children's educational development. Sustained shared thinking occurs:
  "when two or more individuals work together to solve a problem, clarify a concept, evaluate an activity, extend a narrative, etc. Both parties must contribute to the thinking and it must develop and extend the understanding." (The EPPE Report, 2005).
- The essential elements of active listening are:
  - generally, to respect the child as a speaker with something to say
  - specifically, to work out exactly what the child is telling you (which may not be immediately clear).
- You can't listen actively if you think you have all the answers, or if you are only concerned about achieving a particular teaching objective. You have to keep an open mind.

Tips, ideas and activities

- Begin each day by greeting each child individually. Organise your classroom so there are no distractions, for example:
  - other adults deal with parents' enquiries
  - children self-register, then have a few minutes of 'quiet choice time'.

As each child arrives, demonstrate the social listening skills of making eye contact, smiling, and greeting the child by name.

- If the child speaks, focus carefully on the communication to model active listening. As well as listening to what she/he says, make sure that you tune into body language, facial expression, tone of voice and so on. Respond with some genuine acknowledgement (*Gosh!... That's lovely... That's very sad...*). You might want to echo what you understand: *So your dad gave you that as a present?*

- You don't have time to get into a conversation, so if the child wants to continue for too long, apologise politely (*I'm sorry, Polly, but I don't have time to talk now*). But if the conversation needs following up, let Polly see you make a note to talk about it later and stick it on the bulletin board.

- If the child doesn't speak, give a compliment – a comment on anything, from something they're wearing to *What a lovely bright smile today!* Thinking of this tunes you into the child. If she/he responds, listen actively, as described above.

- It is impossible to listen actively all the time – although as time goes on, it should come more naturally. However, the key times for active listening are:
  - whenever you engage in 'sustained shared thinking' with a child or group
  - during directed talk, such as circle time.

You Can... Make children's talk more interesting!

You can't model listening unless children talk to you, rather than you always talking to them. But if we want them to talk productively, rather than just prattle, we have to help open up their language.

Thinking points

- Children learn best from first-hand experience mediated by talk. They need opportunities to try out language to explore and express their ideas. Adults can develop vocabulary by introducing words relevant to the situation and explaining them carefully. But children won't internalise that vocabulary unless they get the chance to use it themselves in a meaningful context.

- Children with poor language are greatly handicapped in exploring and expressing their ideas. Sitting beside them and giving a running commentary provides them with relevant words in context.

Tips, ideas and activities

- In all directed talk or sustained shared thinking, look for ways of encouraging children to talk/work out answers/explain their ideas. Ask open, tentative questions. Three good starters are:
  - *I wonder what/why/how...?*
  - *What/why/how do you think...?*
  - *Has anyone any ideas about what/why/how...?*

  Or try feigning ignorance:
  - *I can't imagine how that happened! What do you think?*
  - *Gosh – that's good! How did you manage to do that?*

  All these techniques convey the fact that you really want to know the child's opinion or tap into their knowledge.

- Acknowledge every answer respectfully, even rather daft ones. Children often say the first thing that comes to mind, but given time and encouragement, they can eventually get there. Try using encouraging responses like:
  - *Hmmm, that's an interesting thing to say. How exactly do you mean?*
  - *Gosh – I'd never thought of that! Can you explain?*
  - *Mmmmm – tell me more about that!*

- With children who *don't* talk, try sitting beside them during an activity they have chosen and mirroring their actions. Give a running commentary – *with lots of long pauses.*
  - *I can see you're putting all the dinosaurs in the bucket. I think I'll try that...My bucket's nearly full...I'm going to tip my dinosaurs out too!... You've got three green ones – I'm going to find three blue ones...Oh, that's clever!*

  Children usually join in. But if they don't, at least you are supplying some language to help them think about what they are doing.

You Can... Encourage children to talk to you

All too often the way adults talk to children closes down their talk, rather than opening it up. But you can't model listening unless children talk to you!

Thinking points

- Many children decide early on not to bother answering questions, because of the risk that they will get an answer wrong and feel bad. If there are silent children in your class, make an extra effort to show your interest.
- There are more ideas in:
  - the *Talk to Me* handbook and whiteboard show (Basic Skills Agency, www.basic-skills.org.uk)
  - *Foundations of Literacy* by Sue Palmer and Ros Bayley (Network Continuum)
  - *How to Talk so Kids will Listen and Listen so Kids will Talk* by Adele Faber and Elaine Mazlish (Scribner).

Tips, ideas and activities

- Avoid closed questions that expect a 'correct' answer. If the child knows the answer, she/he gives it and that's that. If the child doesn't know the answer, that's that again – but the child also feels bad about it.

- Resist the temptation to speed things up by answering or explaining yourself.

- Don't be afraid of silence. Children often need 'thinking time' to work out what they want to say. If you leap in to help them out, you'll ruin their chance of finding their own words. Similarly, if there's a child who always answers, find ways to shush them, for example:
  - Aim your questions at other children (and brook no interruptions).
  - Be direct: *Let's give someone else a chance to answer, Ben. It's polite to give people thinking time.*
  - In group/paired activities, ensure chatty children are together so that quieter souls are not swamped.

- If a child shows you some work, avoid the throwaway: *Oh, that's brilliant!* Instead, give specific (genuine) praise and try to open a dialogue: *I can see you've taken lots of trouble over this. I wonder why you used so much green...?* or *This looks really interesting. Tell me about it.*

- If a child says something silly, don't put them down (see page 15). Assume it is you that's silly, because you can't understand what they are getting at.

- During the conversations that arise naturally with children, don't expect them to speak in sentences, or be grammatically correct. It is much more important that they explore and express their ideas. If a child has difficulty expressing something, just repeat it back to them in sentence form for them to confirm that you have understood (and don't expect them to imitate your sentence in real conversations – save *listen – imitate – innovate* for specific teaching).

You Can... Show that listening activities are fun

Children learn best when they are having fun. And teachers teach best when they are having fun too. So in teaching your class to listen, have as much fun as possible!

Thinking points

- Always remember that children learn through imitation, so if you are enthusiastic about an activity, they will learn to be enthusiastic too. Similarly, if you have a playful attitude to language, listening and learning, they will also be free to be playful – and children are programmed to learn through play.

Tips, ideas and activities

- You want your enjoyment of language, listening and learning to shine through and provide a model for the children. So, whenever you are targeting a particular skill or planning an activity, consider the 'fun factor'. How can you make it fun for yourself and for them?
  - Choose activities, and ways of doing them, that suit you and your personality. Then put yourself in the children's shoes and imagine what would make it more fun for them.
  - Look for the pleasure in any activity and maximise it. Look for the problems and minimise them. This is very obvious advice but when you are teaching, it is easy to get bogged down in targets and objectives, and thus lose sight of the importance of enjoyment and motivation.
  - If something sparks the children's interest, capitalise on it. If something is going really badly, drop it (play a game, have a singsong or read a story instead). Don't worry that it means abandoning a whole load of carefully written plans (they will probably come in handy for another day anyway).

- When there is something you know you have to do but feel uncomfortable about, confront your fears and find a way around them! For instance, some teachers don't like singing in public – but if you are going to teach children songs, you just have to sing. Ease yourself into it gradually, for example:
  - use a CD, like A&C Black's *Music Express* (Foundation Stage), which has good songs anyone can join in with, no matter how limited their vocal range
  - start with simple, very familiar songs that you feel comfortable about.

Above all, concentrate on the children's enjoyment of the activity, rather than on yourself and your perceived inadequacies. As the owner of a pretty awful singing voice, I can assure you that children are the most forgiving of audiences!

You Can... Use your awareness of listening skills to do more of what works

Awareness of the key factors underpinning effective listening makes it easier to integrate them into activities across the curriculum.

Thinking points

- Until about 20 years ago, teachers could assume that, for most children, the listening skills described in this book would be 'caught, not taught'. Children who were brought up by loving carers automatically had the experiences that underpin listening and attention skills (being sung and talked to, moving around relatively freely, sharing everyday domestic experiences with adults, playing outside as they got older). In these circumstances, the only children who didn't learn to listen were those who:
  - for some neurological reason had general or specific problems with responding to sound
  - suffered from emotional deprivation and/or a language-poor home background.
- Now so many children (even those brought up by loving carers) lead a highly sedentary, screen-based existence, teachers must be aware of the factors involved in listening and attention span. Once teachers know what they want, in my experience, they are dab hands at devising ways of getting it.

Tips, ideas and activities

- In Chapters 1 and 2, we have identified the following key factors involved in listening:
  - physical control and coordination
  - discriminating foreground against background sounds
  - discriminating between sounds (especially phonemes)
  - social listening skills, such as eye contact and turn-taking
  - auditory memory
  - imaging skills
  - listening stamina.

  We have also seen that the *listen – imitate – innovate* strategy moves children from receptive to expressive language which:
  - increases their vocabulary
  - helps them internalise the patterns of written language.

- Use the suggestions in the rest of this book to target listening skills through:
  - *child-centred, play-based activities* that draw on children's own instinctive learning drives
  - *directed circle time and paired talk activities* that allow every child to participate as a speaker and a listener
  - *music, song, rhythm and rhyme* to sensitise children to language sounds, focus their attention and help them work as a group
  - *storytelling and reading aloud* – to introduce young children to the pleasures of language
  - *'sustained shared thinking' with other children* which – if it is to be productive – involves both speaking and listening
  - *threading the teaching of listening throughout the school day.*

- If something works, find your own favourite ways of doing more of it. If it doesn't, jettison it – and think of something better.

- Remember that teaching is not about following someone else's rules. It is about knowing what you need to achieve and finding ways to achieve it.

You Can... Use explicit praise to encourage good listening

In learning anything – including how to listen – it helps to know exactly when and how you are succeeding. You can help children along by explicitly praising evidence of good listening skills.

Thinking points

- Praise is one of the most important tools of any teacher, because all children crave attention and positive feedback. If you praise them, they will be anxious to repeat the behaviour. But with something as invisible as listening skills, your praise must be explicit or they won't know what to repeat.
- Praising individual children helps build your teaching rapport. So take particular trouble over children whom you find it difficult to praise. Look for any slight improvement, mentally work out why it is an improvement, and praise it! For instance, today, can you say to any little monster: *Well done for staying still and looking at me while I said that?*
- Praise for a group helps bind that group together, further developing social skills.

Tips, ideas and activities

- When you see a child demonstrating a listening subskill, let them know that you are pleased and why, for example:
  - *You're sitting so well – managing to keep still and controlled – very grown-up indeed!*
  - *I love the way you're making eye contact. It shows you're really tuning into what ____ is saying.*
  - *You're so good at taking turns today! No one's interrupting and we're all concentrating on what the speaker says. Pats on the back all round!*
  - *What a wonderful memory! You've remembered the words exactly. You must have listened very carefully to learn like that.*
  - *How clever of you to listen and imagine so well. You've made a wonderful picture in your head. Who needs TV when you can make your own pictures?*
  - *You could listen for Britain! You've managed to concentrate so well and for so long. I don't think any other children of your age could listen for so long.*
  - *Well done! That's a lovely new word you've learned. You listened carefully and imitated exactly what I said. Let's hear it again!*
  - *What grown-up talking! You've really listened hard and remembered the sentence exactly as I said it – and I loved the different ways you finished it off.*
- Praise children both individually and as groups. Watch out particularly for opportunities to praise children who have problems with listening. The minute you see any progress, explicitly praise it so the child is aware that she/he is moving forwards.

You Can... Improve attention skills through games requiring balance and control

Children are designed by nature to acquire the skills they need through play. So they enjoy games and activities that develop coordination and balance – both are skills that are essential for good listening.

Thinking points

- Don't be afraid to play games lots of times as repetition is critical to developing control. The great thing about games children enjoy is that they want to repeat the activity – so they are collaborating in their learning.
- Once a game is familiar through lots of repetition, children enjoy the novelty of variations. They already know the basic procedure, but can now embed some new ideas into the game by adding a new dimension while still practising the skills involved.
- Don't forget that children's own unstructured, loosely-supervised play is just as important for developing balance and control as teacher-directed activities. Ensure children have plenty of opportunity to run, jump, climb and clamber in a safe, outdoor environment. Boys especially need plenty of rough and tumble play.

Tips, ideas and activities

- Simple Stop-Go games, like 'Dodgems' (see page 7) and 'Musical Statues' combine the opportunity to:
  - make big, free movements while the music plays
  - control the body when the music stops
  - listen carefully.

- Devise variations on Stop-Go games to fit in with your theme. For instance:
  - if you have got an animal theme going, ask children to act like particular animals – moving about when the music is playing, and sleeping or freezing when it stops
  - for a weather theme, children could be the wind – rushing wildly during the music and dropping to the ground when it stops.

- Let children with poor coordination and balance play extra Stop-Go games in a small group with a teaching assistant. This allows focus on specific types of physical control, including the use of equipment as part of the game (for example, climbing up the wall-bars while the music is playing, and freezing when it stops).

- Copying games also allow opportunities for freedom of movement combined with intentional control, such as:
  - 'Follow my Leader'
  - 'Oo-oo-oo I Want to be Like You!' (children move around freely until a signal is given, then copy whatever action you are making).

- In copying games, you can focus on the sorts of movement/ balance you think are particularly appropriate for the group or specific individuals.

You Can... Use games to introduce silence

As well as gaining increasing control over their bodily movements, children need to know how to be quiet on demand. This is a skill to be learned like any other.

Thinking points

- Children who regularly shout out in class, apparently unable to control their behaviour, may never have had any practice of this sort of control. Games are an opportunity to provide that practice, as well as giving everyone the chance to experience silence in a large group.

Tips, ideas and activities

- Play games like 'Grandmother's Footsteps'.
  - The group stands behind a set boundary.
  - The child (or teacher) who is 'It' goes some distance away from the boundary, and faces away from the group.
  - While It's back is turned, the children have to move silently towards It.
  - At any point that It wants to, she/he can swivel round to see them – at which point everyone has to freeze.
  - If It sees anyone move, she/he can send them back to the boundary to start again.
  - The first child to reach and touch It gets to be the next It.

- Children who can count to 12 can play 'What's the Time, Mr Wolf?'
  - One child is Mr Wolf and stands with his/her back to the others, who are some distance away, beyond a boundary.
  - The group calls in chorus, *What's the time, Mr Wolf?* and when he turns, they freeze. Mr Wolf then calls a time, for example, *3 o'clock*. The group silently takes three steps forward, and Mr Wolf turns away again.
  - At any point he can reply *Dinner time!* and chase the group, trying to catch his dinner. They are allowed to squeal as they race back to the safety of the boundary mark.
  - If Mr Wolf catches anyone, they become the next Mr Wolf.

- Children,with a degree of control enjoy 'Sleeping Lions'.
  - Three or four children are hunters. The rest are lions, lying, asleep on the ground, keeping eyes tightly shut.
  - At the teacher's signal, the hunters tiptoe silently among the lions. Each chooses a lion to touch (stroking, tapping, etc) until the teacher gives the signal to withdraw.
  - The lions then sit up. Those who have been touched then guess which hunter touched them. If they get it right, they swap places and become a hunter.

- Once children know the ropes of these games, you can devise variations related to your current themes.

You Can... Use games to develop discriminative listening

Games are an ideal way of helping children learn to discriminate between a widening range of sounds.

Thinking points

- The first three suggestions involve discriminative listening linked to a specific activity – this is important training for following instructions. Children who learn to follow instructions through play, where there is no blame or unpleasant consequence for failure, are more likely to slot easily into the rule-based lifestyle of formal schooling.
- The remaining games all help children discriminate between different sounds, which is the skill required for success in phonics. Again, a playful approach is likely to make more impression on very young children than too early an introduction to formal work. Children who make little progress in formal classwork need more opportunities to play, not fewer.
- Teacher-directed play is very helpful, but child-initiated play is even better. If you can find activities that children really enjoy, elements will seep into their own unstructured play, which is much richer in meaning.

Tips, ideas and activities

- The 'Dodgems' game on page 7 helps children discriminate a foreground sound against background noise. In games like 'Musical Statues' and 'Oo-Oo-Oo I Want to be Like You!' (page 20), you can sometimes swap *When the music stops…* for *When you hear this sound…* as the signal for change.

- The next step up is games where different sounds require different responses, such as 'Traffic Lights' – children move around pretending to be cars until you shout *Red!* (they stop), *Green!* (they can go) or *Amber!* (they slow down).

- To help children learn the importance of listening carefully, play 'Simon Says', where the teacher gives instructions, but children must only follow them if they are preceded by the words 'Simon says'.

- There are lots of commercially-produced games on CD to help children refine their ability to identify and discriminate between a range of sounds. Or you could create your own tape of household sounds for children to:
  - try to identify
  - play 'Sound Bingo', where they match sounds on tape to pictures on bingo cards.

- You can also use the children's own voices. In 'Who's This?', one child sits on a chair facing away from the rest. When you tap one of them on the head they say, *Who's this?* in a loud, clear voice and the child on the chair tries to identify each voice.

- As for games to develop phonemic discrimination, children who are used to language and play are usually only too ready to put the two together. Natural language play includes:
  - making up silly rhymes (It's easy-peasy-lemon-squeezy)
  - clapping, skipping, dipping and playground rhymes
  - nonsense language games ('Chinese Whispers', 'Sausage and Mash')
  - games focusing on initial sounds ('I Spy').

You Can... Use play to encourage social listening

In real life, speaking and listening seldom happen in carefully-structured situations such as organised games, but as part of genuine human interaction. Children practise this real-life interaction through their own child-initiated role-play.

Thinking points

- Ann Locke, an expert in children's language development, sets out this developmental progression for children's talk and learning:
  - *learning from real life* – familiar everyday experiences and routines (learning from 'whole self involvement')
  - *recreating and extending real life* – everyday experience reproduced in pretend activities and imaginative play
  - *real life in the hands* – playing with dolls, soldiers, dinosaurs
  - *life through looking and talking* – making sense of two-dimensional experience (the eyes and the mouth)
  - *unsupported talk about children's own and others' experience* (the mouth alone).

If children have not had opportunities for the first three levels of talk and learning, the more advanced levels are based on very shaky foundations.

Tips, ideas and activities

- Encourage pretend real-life speaking and listening by giving plenty of opportunities for:
  - structured role-play-provide the makings of a well-equipped home area or other themed role-play area (for example, shop, cafe, garage, doctor's or vet's surgery, garden centre, science lab, airport, police station).
  - spontaneous role-play-provide prop-boxes, dressing-up clothes and story-boxes with props for acting out favourite stories.
  - small-scale play-let children create their own 'small worlds', such as towns, farms, prehistoric or alien landscapes, using puppets, toys and anything else to hand. If they are feeling creative, they can create the whole landscape, in a plastic tray, peopled with toy figures, animals and vehicles.

- To take maximum advantage of the speaking and listening opportunities in these play scenarios, children need to know how people/animals/aliens interact in their pretend worlds. The stories you read or tell them can help, or you can join in the pretend play and model the interactions... or why not try ICT? *Early Vision* (www.earlyvision.co.uk) provides short videos of real-life people going about their daily round, speaking and listening to each other. Playing the video a few times familiarises children with the behaviour and language patterns involved, facilitating active speaking and listening in their pretend play.

- While adults can help get the play started, to be truly interactive and valuable, it must be child-centred and child-directed. As long as children are interacting civilly, leave them to it, and let nature take charge of the learning.

You Can... Develop imaging skills through play

Imagination is a key ingredient of play, so games and role-play often help children to create 'pictures in their heads' – this develops the key listening skill of mental imaging.

Thinking points

- The younger (or more immature) the child, the more whole-body movement aids learning, including the learning of mental imaging. A game such as 'Animal Magic' combines this activity with maintaining silence, careful listening and Stop-Go discrimination.
- Every sort of creative play (especially children's own unstructured play) provides opportunities for:
  - developing powers of mental imaging
  - language development and social skills.

However, many 'higher authorities' in primary education see play as an unimportant, frivolous add-on to 'real work'. They *must* be convinced, through careful explanation, of play's significance in underpinning listening, language and learning.

Tips, ideas and activities

- Play games in which children listen to you and mime what you describe. For instance, 'Animal Magic':
  - You need plenty of space for this. Children stand in a space with eyes shut. Explain that you are going to say the name of an animal and give them a minute to imagine how that animal moves.
  - Then say the starting spell, for example:
    Animal magic flee and flow
    Move like a dog – now off you go.
    The children open their eyes and turn into that animal, moving around until they hear the stop signal (bell, whistle, or more magic words if you like).
  - They return to standing with eyes shut, while you give another animal and (after a few moments to think) the starting spell.

- You can play occasional short miming games. For instance:
  - ask children to mime common activities, such as cleaning teeth, putting on a coat or hat, playing football or washing their faces.
  - when asking children to remember an activity they recently performed, ask them to mime it rather than explain verbally (or combine the two).

- Children naturally use mime in role-play, so ensure there are always plenty of role-play opportunities, prop-boxes, dressing-up clothes, etc (see page 23).

- Use plenty of drama activities of all kinds across the curriculum. For instance, use physical theatre, asking children to act out processes like the life cycles of birds, frogs or butterflies; older children could be planets in the solar system, light beams bouncing off or passing through surfaces, and so on.

- Provide plenty of opportunity for loosely supervised, unstructured play, and children will create imaginative scenarios of their own.

You Can... Use play to develop listening stamina

Play is the ideal context in which to develop listening stamina, as children are usually highly motivated to play and will therefore listen for longer periods.

Thinking points

- These games all depend on short-term memory – remembering something for a few minutes, to complete a task. Very often this draws on auditory memory skills (for instance, remembering a phone number, simple directions or instructions). By focusing on listening and remembering in a game, children become more able to remember sequences of sound, which helps in day-to-day, short-term memory tasks.
- Short-term memory also involves visual memory skills which, in many contemporary children, are quite well-developed. Helping children link auditory and visual skills strengthens their short-term memory overall.

Tips, ideas and activities

- With all listening games, start short and sweet, then build up tolerance gradually. Try to stop *before* children lose interest, so they will be highly motivated to play again. Always give plenty of praise for successful play, again to ensure motivation to return.

- Play cumulative listening games, such as:
  - *Mrs Brown went to town and she bought a...*
  - *I went on holiday and I packed a...*
  - *When we went to... we saw a...*

  where each child recites the whole of the list as it stands and adds another item. These are ideal fillers for the odd five minutes, or when on the bus for a school trip.

- With younger (or immature) children, keep cumulative games short, and concentrate on building the skill and congratulating them on their memory skills. With older, more able children, you could:
  - make the lists alphabetical (for example, apple, book, candle), which aids memorisation by providing a form of organisation
  - turn it into a team game (boys against girls is always motivating), and continue until one child can't remember the list – but be careful to keep the poor soul's spirits up!

- Help older children practise the alphabet through games where you go round and each child provides information for one letter, for example:
  - My name is *Alice,* my husband's name is *Alfred.*
  - I went for a ride on an *alligator* and it took me to *Africa.*

- To develop mental imaging, play 'Kim's Game' (where you show children a number of items on a tray, then remove it from sight and they have to remember all the items). Over time, gradually increase the number of items displayed. Most people also find that saying the names of items aloud (which provides an auditory echo) helps with memory. With older children, demonstrate how categorisation can help memory; in other words, linking together in your mind all the items that have something in common . Again, saying the groups aloud usually aids memorisation.

You Can... Use circle activities to build listening stamina

Circle time is ideal for building listening stamina. In fact, unless you target this skill, many circle time activities can be ruined by children's inability to attend.

Thinking points

- If children have poor attention skills, circle time can easily deteriorate into chaos. Children who have not yet had a turn or those who have already spoken lose interest and start misbehaving. In a large circle of 30 children, the teacher may have to spend all her time on crowd control, trying to keep sections of the circle on task. This is not only a waste of the teacher's time and energy; it is also positively counter-productive because children are learning *not* to listen to each other.

- Some teachers are reluctant to work with a small group, thinking that the rest of the class might get up to mischief. If, however, by working with small groups you develop children's listening and attention skills, there should be a lot less mischief in the future.

Tips, ideas and activities

- Don't expect very young children (or older children with attention problems) to be able to listen for more than a couple of minutes to begin with. Try this introductory circle time on the first day of term – just you and, say, four to six children:
  - Demonstrate how to make eye contact with the person beside you, shake hands and introduce yourself, for example, *Hello, my name is Mrs Palmer.*
  - Each child then makes eye contact and shakes hands with the next person, repeating the formula but substituting their own name.
  - Praise the children individually for their performance, especially the way they listen when not actually personally involved.

Repeat this activity with all the children in small groups, while the rest of the class get on with some work or have free time.

- Make a note of those children who have difficulty attending. The next day you can adjust the size of the circle so that:
  - children who found it difficult might be in a smaller group
  - those who found it easy to attend and participate could be in a slightly bigger group (which will take longer).

- Do very short circle times every day for a week or so (see the rest of this section for ideas) until the majority of the class is able to function in one or two large circles. Children who are still experiencing difficulty need extra help – and this is well worth an investment of time and teaching. The *Spirals* course (*Language Development: Circle Time Sessions to Improve Communication Skills* by Marion Nash, Jackie Lowe and Tracey Palmer (David Fulton)) can be run by a teaching assistant with a small group.

You Can... Use circle activities to teach social listening

Circle time is all about social listening. It is the perfect place to rehearse and revise the social skills you want children to use throughout the school day.

Thinking points

- Don't feel you have to provide different activities for each circle time. Remember the importance of repetition in young children's learning. You can use a quick activity like passing a look round the circle many times, but it helps to make slight variations (as suggested opposite) to keep the children interested.
- Circle time often focuses on combining Personal, Social and Emotional education with speaking and listening, but it can also be an opportunity to link to other curricular areas, particularly in terms of introducing new vocabulary and language structures.

Tips, ideas and activities

- Circle time is an ideal opportunity to model social listening, and to convey to children that good listening is as important as good talking. Make sure the children are very clear about rules (use visual cue cards to remind them when they forget – see page 47 and photocopiable page 61), and make sure your circle is the right size (see page 26). You can then use circle time as an opportunity to home in on all the social listening skills.

- For instance, one of the best ways to help children make eye contact is to 'pass a look around the circle'. You can do this as a regular opening for your circle time. Ring the changes by:
  - turning it into a wink, a smile or a compliment.
  - suggesting particular facial expressions (happy, sad, shocked, proud and so on).

The circle activity on page 26 can also be used as an opening gambit on other occasions, helping children to learn the important social skill of introducing themselves.

- Circle time combines turn-taking with opportunities for imitation and repetition. For instance, with younger children, you could play 'Toy Shop', using pictures of toys cut from a catalogue. Put the pictures in the middle of the circle and explain to the children that they are going to pretend they are visiting the toy shop and can choose any toy they would like. Model the language (*My name is... and I am choosing a...*) Support children who need it by putting in the language for them – with practice, they will soon be joining in. Try the game with colours, fruit, clothes or any other topic you may be covering.

- Put great emphasis on the importance of active listening (see page 14) in circle time activities. Show by your own body language and responses how closely you focus on what each speaker is saying, and expect everyone in the circle to listen actively as well (encourage children to respond to contributions, as long as they put their hand up first). Congratulate children on active listening.

- There are many suggestions for activities at various levels in
  - the Lucky Duck materials – www.luckyduck.co.uk
  - Jenny Moseley's Quality Circle Time materials – www.circle-time.co.uk

You Can... Use circle time to develop imaging skills

There are many reasons to encourage children to 'see pictures in their heads' in circle time, and they tend to be quiet, restful activities – ideal for developing a range of listening skills.

Thinking points

- Mental imaging is an established technique for stress-management, so highly relevant to the PSE function of circle time. Many children today lead fairly frantic, chaotic lives, so it can be helpful to them to have safe or calm places to retreat to if necessary in their heads. Once they have acquired the technique, some teachers might be able to integrate it into strategies for anger management or conflict resolution.
- These activities require a quiet environment, so if only part of the class is in the circle, you will have to find somewhere to take them away from noise – or use a time when the other half are perhaps playing outdoors.

Tips, ideas and activities

- Use circle time for asking children to use their imaginations. Make sure they are sitting comfortably on chairs, then ask them to close their eyes and imagine that it is the end of the school day: *You're feeling very tired and you just want to get home and have a nice rest. Think about a special place in your house where you'll go for a rest.* Give them a few moments to decide, then say: *In your head, imagine yourself going through the door into your house and going to your special place. Can you see it? Settle down in your special place and feel all cosy. Think about what you can see around you... what you can hear... what you can smell... what you can feel against your skin?* Finally, ask children to open their eyes and go round the circle, saying a couple of sentences about their special place. You model it first (*My special place at home is my sofa. It's red with big, soft cushions. I like to snuggle there with my dog*).

- On another occasion, find a piece of restful music (such as Grieg's *Morning* or Saint-Saens' *The Swan*). Ask the children to think of lovely, quiet places they would like to visit when they are angry or frightened – a beach, a woodland, a beautiful room – somewhere safe, calm and restful. Go round the circle asking for suggestions. Then ask children to think of a special place for themselves, close their eyes and, when the music starts, imagine themselves in their calm place. Play the music for as long as appropriate for their level of listening stamina – don't let them get restless. Try to create a magical, restful feeling. In another circle time, let the children revisit their calm place. You could then use the music on occasions when you want to calm the class, or create a quiet atmosphere.

- There are many visualisation activities you can adapt from *Circle Time Activities for Relaxation and Imagination* by Tony Pryce (Lucky Duck Publishing).

You Can... Develop literate language

Circle time is a great opportunity for using the listen – imitate – innovate technique to familiarise children with the rhythms and patterns of written language.

Thinking points

- Abstract concepts like 'sentence' are meaningless to young children, so explanations ('Starts with a capital, ends with a full stop, makes complete sense') are a waste of time. But the repeated use of the word within a meaningful context helps children get a 'feel' for what a sentence is, especially as they then hear – and articulate – a particular sentence structure.

Tips, ideas and activities

- Use circle time to introduce children to the concept of 'a sentence' gradually and naturally, without any explicit teaching. Whenever you intend to use a sentence frame, introduce the session with the words *We're going to say a sentence today.* This allows children to hear the term 'sentence' within a meaningful context, and is much more likely to help them understand the concept over time than a decontexualised explanation such as *A sentence makes complete sense.*

- With young children, use short, simple sentences. Say the beginning of the sentence, and then raise your arm to show you are giving *your* particular sentence ending. For instance: *My favourite time at school is* (raise arm) *circle time.* Ensure the first few children to speak after you have good auditory memories so they will give a good, clear rendition. As the sentence frame goes round the circle, the less able children will hear it repeated many times and have a better chance of internalising the frame. After *listening*, they have the option of *imitating* or *innovating*, for example, *My favourite time at school is break.*

- With older children, you can use more complex sentence constructions, for example:
  - *My favourite time at school is... because...*
  - *When I get home, the first thing I do is...*
  - *If I feel sad, I like to...*
  - *The best thing about spring is that...*

  If there is a particular sort of construction you want to cover in children's literacy work, you could introduce it via a circle time activity of this kind.

- For many children, structured opportunities such as these may be the only times they actually speak in complete sentences. It is therefore essential to recognise the importance of the *listen – imitate – innovate* model in underpinning children's success as writers, and finding ways to integrate it into teaching across the curriculum.

You Can... Develop ability to keep a steady beat

Developing children's sense of rhythm helps them with every sort of listening. The ability to keep a steady beat has particular importance for children's educational success.

Thinking points

- Research has shown that the ability to keep a steady beat is one of the most significant indicators of children's success at school. Beat competence is connected with:
  - bodily coordination and control
  - the patterning of information in the brain
  - overall listening skills.
- Auditory memory depends to a large extent on beat competence: think of the way you use beat in reciting the numbers 1–100, the alphabet, the months of the year, and so on.
- All activities involving music, song, rhythm and rhyme help develop beat competence. A teacher in Finland, where music and song are threaded throughout the school day, explained to me that 'Music trains the mind to pattern and the ears to sound'. Spot on!

Tips, ideas and activities

- Use steady beat activities such as:
  - 'Copycat': You model a simple beat (clapping hands, tapping knees, etc) and ask the children as a group to copy you. When they have got the hang of it, ask individuals to tap a beat for other children to copy.
  - 'Chopsticks': Give each child a paper plate and a chopstick, and sit them in a circle. Ask one child to use the chopstick to tap a simple rhythm on the plate, and then get the others to copy it. Develop 'chopstick conversations' where one child (or half the group) taps out a rhythm, and another child (or the other half of the group) taps a 'reply'.

- Teach – or encourage – the children to make up simple raps. Get the class performing these with plenty of body movement, clapping, etc.

- Early Years specialist Ros Bayley has developed many materials for steady beat activities, including her popular Beat Baby resources, Action Raps and a book: *Helping Young Children Keep a Steady Beat*. All are available from Lawrence Educational Publications (01922 643833 and www.educationalpublications.com).

- Use the following types of activity to develop beat competence:
  - marching, dancing, clapping and skipping games
  - traditional songs and nursery rhymes
  - playground rhymes and chants.

Almost every musical activity involves a steady beat. Encourage children's awareness by clapping and moving rhythmically yourself.

You Can... Develop coordination through music

Blending words, rhythm, music and actions helps children develop bodily control, balance and attention span. All of these are essential if children are to be able to sit still and listen.

Thinking points

- When a baby is born, there are few connections between the two sides of the brain. Gradually – as a result of childhood experiences – neural pathways are forged through the *corpus callosum*, the bundle of nerves connecting left and right hemispheres. Children need strong connections between the left hemisphere (where the brain processes words, linear sequences and pattern) and the right (specialising in holistic patterning, spatial awareness and music). Action songs, marching songs, clapping and skipping rhymes are all great – and natural – ways of promoting connections between the hemispheres.
- In the past, the sorts of activities listed above were common practice throughout the day in infant schools, but in recent years there has been a tendency to concentrate instead on more academic approaches. And yet, in a world where children's listening and coordination skills are not developing naturally, this sort of fun musical activity is more essential than ever.

Tips, ideas and activities

- Regularly sing action songs which help children develop physical coordination and control, for example:
'Heads and Shoulders, Knees and Toes'
'Row, Row, Row your Boat'
'If you're Happy and you Know it'
'Incy Wincy Spider'
'Wind the Bobbin up'
'There was a Princess Long Ago'
'The Wheels on the Bus'
'One Finger, One Thumb Keep Moving'
Make up your own songs to go with themes you are covering, or to help children remember facts. Choose a familiar, easy tune and put your own words and actions to it.

- Teach children some simple marching songs, such as 'The Grand Old Duke Of York'. Make up your own songs for marching too, to fit in with themes or the time of year. Then sing and march – in the playground, down the school corridors to lunch or the hall, and anywhere you go in the great outdoors. Take musical instruments to help keep the beat and add to the fun.

- Teach children some simple dances, such as the 'Hokey Cokey'. Children also love learning popular cult dances, including old favourites like 'The Chicken Song' and 'YMCA'. Teach local folk dances (or maypole dances) too.

- Encourage clapping games and rhymes. These are excellent for coordination skills, and many include cross-over movements that help make connections between the two sides of the brain. There are lots of examples in Jenny Moseley's book, *Clapping Games* (Positive Press). You can also see clapping and other action rhymes demonstrated on the CBeebies programme *Razzledazzle* (www.bbc.co.uk/cbeebies/razzledazzle).

- Encourage children to learn to skip and to chant skipping rhymes, such as *Salt, mustard, vinegar, pepper* or the old cherry-counting chant: *Tinker, tailor, soldier, sailor, rich man, poor man, beggarman, thief.*

You Can... Develop children's social listening

Singing, chanting rhymes or moving to music together is an extremely social activity, helping children literally to work in harmony – listening to each other, taking turns and tuning their own bodily and vocal activity to that of the group.

Thinking points

- Since time immemorial, human beings have used music, rhythm and song to socialise their young. Not only do these songs, dances and marches develop the individual's coordination, they help children learn to coordinate their own actions with those of the group. They may look like a bit of fun (and they are) but they have an extremely important purpose.
- Singing and chanting together are also good ways to memorise words. To start with, the children with good auditory memories carry the others. Gradually, as the words become more familiar, everyone begins to remember them. However, the many children who now come to school without the old repertoire of nursery rhymes will need lots of repetitive practice to catch up. Sometimes they can appear to be reciting in a group, but when you hear them individually they are gliding over many of the words. So do make sure you listen to children individually as well as in chorus.

Tips, ideas and activities

- Start each day with a 15-minute 'Song and Rhyme Time', during which the children:
  - practise their song/rhyme for the week (see page 35)
  - revisit a few old favourites, or ones that cover information you are teaching, such as alphabet, counting or tables songs
  - take occasional requests.

This is a good way to start the day, as it settles children and sets their brains and bodies working in a social, patterned way.

- Don't worry if you are not much of a singer yourself – the children won't notice! But it is essential that you (and all adults in the classroom) set a good example by joining in with gusto.

- As children become proficient at singing and reciting, create 'conversations' by splitting the class in half and giving each half a section to sing/recite. Start with simple echoing songs such as 'I Hear Thunder' (see photocopiable page 57), and then adapt other songs and rhymes.

- With older children, you might progress to simple rounds. 'I Hear Thunder' can, of course, be sung as a round because it uses the tune of 'Frère Jacques'. But it is better to start with something simpler, such as 'Animal Fair'.

- Marching also develops social skills, involving moving in concert with other people. This is one of the reasons the armed forces place so much store by marching – it helps forge a sense of belonging to the group. Once the children have got the hang of it, you can teach them simple routines, such as marching singly, joining into pairs, then into fours … and peeling off into pairs again. Teach simple dances too – these are highly collaborative, and the constant repetition helps lay down strong neural networks upon which future collaborative endeavours can be built.

- There are further suggestions for using music, songs and rhymes to develop collaboration in the class's daily routine on page 46.

You Can... Use music to develop sound discrimination

All music-making develops children's appreciation of sound, so ensure there are plenty of opportunities for child-initiated and teacher-directed musical activities.

Thinking points

- Music is the obvious vehicle for developing listening skills of all kinds, but particularly discriminative listening. Children's own experimentation is the best way to develop an interest in sounds.
- Making music involves remembering sequences of sounds, which is an important aspect of auditory memory, especially in literacy. For instance, when children start to read, they have to remember sequences of phonemes, starting with short consonant–vowel–consonant sequences (for example, c-a-t), but building up longer ones (for example, c-r-u-n-ch). Later, when spelling, they will need to hold sequences of syllables in their heads (for example, mul-ti-syll-ab-ic).

Tips, ideas and activities

- Provide music areas (both inside and outdoors), where children can go to explore sound. Provide instruments that can be beaten, shaken, blown or strummed. Collect objects and materials (such as recycled household objects and packaging) which the children can use to make their own musical instruments. When children are working with music-making equipment, take every opportunity to use the language of sound (pitch: *high*, *low*; volume: *soft*, *loud*, etc). Help them notice the difference between long-drawn out sounds and short, jerky sounds. All of these provide practice in sound discrimination.

- Provide a listening centre where children can go to listen to a range of music, and take advantage of any opportunity for the children to hear adults and older children singing and playing instruments.

- Use musical sounds as replacements for simple instructions; for example, tapping a triangle as a signal for silence, tapping out a rhythm on a drum when it is time to line up and so on.

- Use instruments for this memory game. You need two sets of the same small instruments (for example, drum, rattle, triangle, shaker, chime bar).
  - Put one set in front of a screen of some kind and the other behind it.
  - Using the instruments *behind* the screen, play a sequence of sounds, setting the instruments down in sequence as you do so (start with two and build up as children become more skilful). Remove any unused instruments.
  - Now ask the children to identify the instruments they heard and place them in front of the screen in the correct sequence.
  - Then remove the screen. The children will have immediate feedback about the accuracy of their choice. Talk about any wrong choices and why they might have happened.

- Encourage children to use instruments to make up their own short musical sequences, and play them repeatedly.

You Can... Use songs and rhymes to alert children to phonemes

Children have traditionally learned the sounds of their language through nursery rhymes and songs. Nowadays, it is more important than ever that we introduce them to this cultural heritage.

Thinking points

- The phonemes of English (as defined by the National Literacy Strategy) are given on page 56.
- Children learn to discriminate the phonemes of their native language in the first year of their lives, through listening to their parents or carers. Throughout history, parents have used songs and rhymes to soothe tiny infants, and these tended to emphasise the phonemes (for example, '*B*ye *B*aby *B*unting', '*D*ance to your *D*addy'). However, since the advent of all-day TV, parents have spent less time talking and singing to their tiny children. This means many children arrive at school with poor phonemic discrimination, and they need plenty of singing and rhyming activities to open their ears to the sounds of language
- Traditional rhymes and songs are also particularly memorable for children. Indeed, this is why they have lasted through the ages – young human beings are programmed to enjoy the things that are good for them.

Tips, ideas and activities

- With four- to six-year-olds, make sure your 'Song and Rhyme Time' (see page 32) includes plenty of nursery rhymes and songs, and practise them very frequently. Every so often, have a 'Nursery Rhyme Festival' when you take the children through their whole repertoire.

- Don't try to introduce more than one song or rhyme at a time (one a week is fine), as repetition is critically important. It may seem to you that you have done a particular rhyme to death, but as long as the children are still enjoying it, keep on singing or saying it.

- One lovely way to focus on nursery rhymes is to make a Nursery Rhyme video, on which the children recite rhymes while acting them out. Use a few simple costumes and props to give it a bit of sparkle, and then find someone who can edit it and put it on DVD. Invite parents along to the 'premiere', to watch the DVD and see their child awarded an Oscar for his or her appearance. You could then sell copies of the DVD for school funds – a great way of returning knowledge of the old rhymes into the home.

- There are many great collections of nursery rhymes and songs, playground and counting rhymes in the Barefoot Books range (www.barefootbooks.com).

- As children get older, their interest in nursery rhymes tends to wane, but they still enjoy short, playful, alliterative rhymes – indeed, playground culture has always been full of them. Many of these (such as 'Slobberdobber Custard, Green Slop Pie') may not be suitable for classroom use, but they are so attractive to children that they will learn them for fun anyway. Two I have found particularly popular are 'Julius Caesar, the Roman Geezer' and 'Nobody Likes Me, Everybody Hates Me' (see page 57).

You Can... Use rhymes and songs to improve children's auditory memory

Rhymes and songs are the best vehicle for developing auditory memory because they are fun to repeat. Children enjoy the sounds of the patterned language, the feeling of the rhythm and the satisfaction of acquisition.

Thinking points

- Remember that repetition, repetition, repetition is the best way to learn anything. Repeating a sequence of words, rhythm and actions (in an action song or rhyme) is particularly powerful. Copying you as you perform an action song or rhyme also draws on that other important human learning strategy, imitation.
- Once children have memorised a song or rhyme, they enjoy singing or reciting it, so more repetition happens naturally – this helps to lay down strong neural networks that will stand them in good stead for further auditory memory work. Treat auditory memory as a kind of mental muscle that needs constant exercising to become strong and efficient.

Tips, ideas and activities

- Start developing auditory memory from the moment children arrive in your class by teaching them rhymes and songs (see page 32 and photocopiable page 57). Make sure they learn one new rhyme or song per week. (I know I keep emphasising this, but it is essential to the development of auditory memory – in the past, children acquired a repertoire of rhymes and songs naturally, but nowadays we have to help them along.)

- The choice of songs and rhymes depends on the age and needs of the children, but should include:
  - teaching songs/rhymes, such as alphabet and tables songs or chants, and those you have made up yourself to teach particular facts
  - traditional songs and nursery rhymes
  - rhymes that emphasise particular phonemes (see page 56)
  - favourites suggested by the children.

- Have a certain time every week (either Monday or Friday) when you introduce the new rhyme or song, and practise it a few times together. Provide a photocopied version for children to take home so that parents can help too (see page 58 – 'Letter to parents 1').

- Use your 'Song and Rhyme Time' for daily practice, and provide a regular 'Performance Time' (perhaps around the middle of the week) for children to take the limelight and recite or sing as individuals, pairs or groups. The opportunity to show off one's skills is a powerful motivator – it also gives you the opportunity to hear individual children performing, and to assess their auditory memory skills.

- Once children know a rhyme well, you can play about with it – for instance, seeing if they can 'spot the deliberate mistake' when you change the words, making up a new version, or playing a game where you start off a rhyme for children (in teams) to finish.

You Can... Use songs and rhymes for listen–imitate–innovate

As children become increasingly sensitive to rhyme and rhythm, they are ready to start playing with these aspects of language themselves.

Thinking points

- Children who are ready to start learning phonics engage in the Humpty-Dumpty type of nonsense-rhyming activity automatically. They make up silly rhymes like 'This is easy-peasy-deasy-weasy' or 'This picture is Mr Ooly-Wooly-Pooly'. It is an indication that they have begun to notice the opening sounds of words (onset) and their final sounds (rimes). There are many ways you can use innovations on rhymes and songs for learning across the curriculum and classroom management (see page 46). Every time you do so, you help strengthen the neural networks you have laid down through music, song, rhyme and rhythm activities.

Tips, ideas and activities

- Use a familiar rhyme, such as 'Humpty Dumpty'. During 'Rhyme Time' one day, provide a variation, such as:
Humpty Dumpty sat on a tree
Humpty Dumpty got stung by a bee
All the king's horses and all the king's men
Couldn't make Humpty better again.
(Variations don't need to be clever – children find almost any innovation amusing.) Offer other first lines and ask children to come up with rhyming conclusions (*Humpty Dumpty sat on a log... sat on a chair... sat on the floor... sat on a pin...* etc).

- Innovate on songs too. Instead of the 'Mulberry Bush', you could go round the Christmas tree, or the roundabout. 'Old MacDonald' could have a shop or a zoo or a school instead of a farm. Or instead of 'Ten Green Bottles, Hanging on the Wall', you could sing about 'Ten Tired Teddies, Sitting on the Bed' (*...and if one tired teddy fell off and banged his head...*). Make use of the rhythmic patterns your children have internalised as vehicles to rehearse ideas and vocabulary from all areas of the curriculum.

- Once you have modelled the idea of innovation, encourage children to come up with their own nonsense versions of favourite songs.

- Perhaps you could compile your own classroom anthology of 'new versions' of rhymes and songs. This could be taped or video-recorded, or written down and illustrated. Children could then teach their versions to other children, parents, etc.

- For lots of fun activities involving onset and rime, look at *Pat and Co* by Colin and Jacqui Hawkins (www.patandpals.com).

You Can... Use music to develop mental imaging

Listening to music can help all of us conjure up moods and pictures. Let children respond to music through movement, talk and art in order to develop the capacity to 'see pictures in their heads'.

Thinking points

- Modern children have the same problem creating mental images to go with music, as they do with words – TV always provides the pictures, so children have not learned to do it themselves. But if you help them to use movement as a vehicle for developing mental imagery, they have the added power of the kinaesthetic learning channel.

Tips, ideas and activities

- Make a collection of 'programme' music that tells stories or paints pictures – happy, sad, wild, serene, clumsy, graceful. Well-known programme music popular with children includes *Peter and the Wolf, The Carnival of the Animals, The Flight of the Bumble Bee, The Sugar Plum Fairy* and so on.

- Introduce the children to this music in the school hall, and encourage them to move to it, conveying how it makes them feel. For instance, you could play extracts from two contrasting pieces, such Grieg's *Morning* and *The Hall of the Mountain King.* Ask them why the different music made them feel and move differently. If they are responsive, move on to *I wonder if anyone got any pictures in their head when they were listening to those tunes?*

- When you find a tune that conjures up strong images for children, return to it another time so they can move to it again. On another occasion, ask them to close their eyes as you play it and try to see the pictures in their head. (When asking children to listen to music without moving to it, remember to start with only a short extract and gradually build listening tolerance.)

- Choose another tune children enjoy as a stimulus for art work. Again, give the chance to move first, then provide painting or modelling materials and let them convey the pictures in their heads.

- Use restful, gentle music alongside circle time imaging activities to help children conjure up their own special world. If a certain tune becomes associated with this sort of calming activity, you might find it helpful as a way of calming the class when disruption has made them fractious.

You Can... Develop listening stamina with music, songs and rhymes

For young children, familiarity doesn't breed contempt. As long as they are enjoying themselves, familiarity breeds security, success and staying power. So singing favourite songs or listening to favourite tunes over and over again helps develop listening stamina and increases their attention span.

Thinking points

- To adults, repetition is boring – we constantly seek variety and innovation. For young children, however, it is essential for the creation of strong neural networks, into which further learning can be slotted.
- Before the availability of TV, video and so on, babies and toddlers were exposed to a great many repetitions of songs and rhymes – it was the only resource their parents had to comfort or entertain them. Over time, children would gradually pick up the tunes and words themselves and join in.
- Many parents today buy their children a video or tape of songs, rather than singing themselves. But electronic entertainment is essentially passive – without the real-life interaction.
- Most parents, in the past, had a fairly limited repertoire, which was actually an advantage, as it meant more of the repetition their children needed.Nowadays, adults raised in a multimedia world crave variety, and assume that their children do too. DVD, videos, websites, etc provide that variety but the result is less repetition, and less robust neural networks in children's brains.

Tips, ideas and activities

- Teach children number rhymes and cumulative songs involving lots of repetition, such as:
'Old MacDonald'
'There were Ten in a Bed'
'This Old Man, He Played One'
'One Man Went to Mow'
'Five Little Speckled Frogs'
'Green Grow the Rushes-oh'
You will probably find that they will happily go on singing such songs long after you have lost interest! They also enjoy songs like 'The Bear Went over the Mountain' (see page 57) that just go on and on and on... Grit your teeth, and let them sing! You can also make use of their enthusiasm to fill in time on long bus journeys or when the class is obliged to wait around for any reason.

- Familiarity breeds attention skills in terms of music too. If you want children to listen to and enjoy a piece of music, arrange for them to hear it many times before actually 'introducing' it. For instance, you could play it in the background as they arrive in the morning or are getting ready for home. Then, when it is well embedded, talk to them about it and invite them to actually listen – perhaps for a purpose such as imaging or art work, or perhaps just for the pleasure of active listening. The more they have been exposed to the music beforehand, the longer they will be able to sit and concentrate on it.

You Can... Target listening while developing children's love of books

The Read-Aloud, Read-Along, Read-Alone technique with picture books introduces children to the pleasure of reading – and develops listening skills on the side.

Thinking points

- Read-Aloud, Read-Along, Read-Alone is not a way of teaching children to read – it is a way of introducing them to books and developing their memory skills and appreciation of various aspects of written language. It can be done at any age. However, many lucky children through the ages *have* learned to read through RA-RA-RA at home, when a parent or other beloved adult shared favourite picture books with them. And if a child has good listening skills (including discriminative listening), it is possible to 'pick up' phonics through repeated pleasurable interactions with books.
- Most children today, however, need help to develop discriminative listening. They also need explicit teaching of phonics. Once this begins, it can proceed alongside RA-RA-RA. As they gradually develop:
  - an understanding of the alphabet code
  - the ability to decode words for themselves

  many children will begin to see how their phonic knowledge applies to the words they 'read alone' in RA-RA-RA sessions.

Tips, ideas and activities

- Make a collection of picture books suitable for reading aloud, so children will read along (and eventually 'read' alone). As you introduce these to the children, keep them in a special RA-RA-RA box. They should be enjoyable 'quick reads' with repetitive, rhythmic or patterned language (see photocopiable page 60 for suggestions). Have daily story sessions when you read:
  - the Book of the Week (a featured picture book that you read every day to build up children's familiarity)
  - one book with which the children are already familiar
  - one book requested by the children.

  With young children, you might have two or three story sessions scattered through the day, each fairly short. As you build children's listening stamina, you might prefer to move towards one main session. Don't attempt to 'teach reading' in these sessions – your main aims are:
  - to have fun and develop children's interest and delight in sharing books you read aloud
  - to encourage them to read along and, gradually, to hand the 'reading' over to the children.

- Buy duplicate copies of your RA-RA-RA books (a few of each title, if possible) for children to take home and share with parents. Explain the principles of RA-RA-RA to parents so they – and other adults – can share books in the same way at home (see the letter on photocopiable page 59).

You Can... Develop auditory memory skills through RA-RA-RA

Read-Aloud, Read-Along, Read-Alone is the perfect vehicle for developing auditory memory, and many texts also familiarise children with common written language patterns.

Thinking points

- Children know instinctively that they *need* lots of repetition to develop their language skills – this is why every child has a favourite story that they want to hear again and again. Parents reading the same bedtime story for the fiftieth time can be driven almost demented by this instinctive need! But to develop children's auditory memory at school, teachers also have to put up with the same levels of repetition.
- 'Read-Alone' in the early stages is, of course, just reciting. Many adults think this is somehow 'cheating', which is why parents and others need to have the significance of auditory memory explained to them. Many of the books children learn by heart through RA-RA-RA will be written in sentences, thus giving oral practice of written language patterns.

Tips, ideas and activities

- When you introduce the Book of the Week on Monday, read it at least twice. After the first reading, children may like to talk about the pictures and story before they hear it again. On the second reading, start encouraging them to Read-Along.

- Children usually join in naturally, but if not, try the following techniques:
  - If it is a repetitive text, look expectantly at the children when repetition occurs – there are usually one or two children with good memories who will get the reading along off the ground.
  - If it is a rhyming text, pause before the rhyming words to give children the chance to supply them.
  - If it is prose, try pausing slightly in the middle of a sentence to see if they can finish it off.
  - With difficult-to-remember sections, find a sing-song, rhythmic way of reading the words, and encourage children to use it too.
  - Ask children to help make up actions to remind you of certain sections.

As children get to know the book over the course of the week, expect the more skilful children to lead the others in joining in more and more. Aim for the whole class to be reciting the whole Book of the Week by Friday.

- If you then return regularly to books in your RA-RA-RA box, the children will build up a repertoire of books they can recite from memory. When they have a reasonable grasp of phonics, they can return to these books and apply their newly-won skills as they read alone. The familiarity of the RA-RA-RA texts will help them integrate phonic decoding with prediction and the recognition of common 'sight words' that cannot be decoded phonetically.

You Can... Use storytelling to develop listening skills

Since time immemorial, adults have taught children how to listen by telling them stories. Pie Corbett has devised a way of using this age-old technique to develop auditory memory and prepare children to write their own stories.

Thinking points

- Over a school year, you could teach children five or six stories in this way. As well as developing their language and listening skills, you are filling their heads with characters, settings and plots – and ways to express them – ready for when they come to write stories for themselves.
- The technique makes use of the two key learning strategies of imitation and repetition, while the use of actions, story-maps, puppets and prop-boxes supports learning through visual and kinaesthetic channels.
- For more information and many other good ideas, see Pie Corbett's *Bumper Book of Storytelling into Writing Key Stage 1* (Clown Publishing – available on Amazon).

Tips, ideas and activities

- As a change from RA-RA-RA now and then, have storytelling sessions for a week, using Pie Corbett's technique.
- Choose a repetitive children's story you know well, such as:
'The Three Little Pigs'
'The Gingerbread Man'
'The Three Bears'
'The Three Billy Goats Gruff'
'The Little Red Hen'
'The Enormous Turnip'
- Work out your own version of the story, including devising actions to accompany it. Then practise telling your story (with the actions) a few times until you feel fluent. Make a picture 'story-map' showing the main events of the story in sequence (this doesn't have to be grand – stick figures and rough squiggles are actually better than a smart visual representation: see page 10).
- Tell the story, with actions, during your Monday storytime session. Then repeat it, a line at a time, asking the children to imitate you (in both words and actions). Display your story-map, so children have an overview of the whole thing, and then tell the whole story again, asking the children to join in.
- Tell the story a couple of times every day, aiming for them to learn it by heart within a few days. After several practices, take away your story-map and ask them to make their own. You could also provide puppets and prop-boxes so that children can act out the story, during free time.
- Once children have a reasonable grasp of the story, get them to practise in pairs, facing each other, as well as in the whole group. Ask some of the word-perfect children to take over your place and lead the group.

You Can... Use storytelling to develop literate language

Storytelling is like a bridge between spoken and written language. Pie Corbett uses it to familiarise children with sentence structures and useful written vocabulary such as connectives.

Thinking points

- Children who do a lot of RA-RA-RA will meet many useful written language patterns, but your own story-telling is an opportunity to target specific useful words and language structures. Choose the sort of words, phrases and sentence frames you want children to use in their own writing in the future.
- As evidence of pupil progress, try Pie Corbett's method of assessment. He simply selects three children before he starts (an able, middle and lower ability child) and asks them to tell a story into a tape-recorder. Then he repeats the procedure at the end – the difference in language ability and confidence, especially for middle and lower ability pupils, is startling.

Tips, ideas and activities

- You can use storytelling as an opportunity to introduce some of the language features children need for *writing* stories. If they learn these language features orally first, they will have them as auditory echoes in their heads when they come to write.

- Think of your story as having four distinct parts, each with certain key language features:
  - *introduction* (giving essential background, including the main character(s): *Once upon a time, there was/were... who lived in/near...*)
  - *the start-up*, when events begin to happen (*Early one morning/One fine day/One dark stormy night*)
  - *the main story*, when repetitive events build up to a climax (this is the longest section of the story, using time connectives like *then, next, meanwhile, eventually* and other useful connectives such as *unfortunately*)
  - *the ending* when everything is resolved (using time connectives like *finally, at last* and problem-solving connectives such as *fortunately, luckily*).

- When devising actions to go with your story, use special actions to highlight these key language features, for instance:
  - put one arm in the air every time you use a time connective
  - put both arms in the air whenever you use a problem-solving connective
  - make a left-to-right rippling movement with your hand when you use a word that introduces an extra 'chunk' of information into a sentence, such as *who, while, whenever.*

Use the same actions for specific sorts of words and structures every time you tell a story.

You Can... Use storytime to develop sound discrimination

It is fun to make sound effects to illustrate the stories you read and tell, and this provides opportunities for children to think about and discriminate between sounds.

Thinking points

- Linking stories, drama and music can also help develop mental imaging (see next page).
- The more explicit you are in talking about sound effects, the more you alert children to the qualities of sound. This helps them to discriminate more effectively. It also provides them with vocabulary to talk about sound themselves.
- There are many more practical ideas in, *Music from Storybooks* by Ali McCLure (Out of the Ark Books).

Tips, ideas and activities

- When reading or telling stories, ask children to help you choose the best voices, for instance a high-pitched voice for an elf or a little child, and low-pitched, gruff tones for a giant or ogre. Invite the children to vary tone, pitch and quality of voice when they join in with recitation and tell stories.

- When a story or book is familiar, try creating a choral presentation with sound effects. This activity works particularly well with books containing a lot of onomatopoeic sounds, such as *We're Going on a Bear Hunt* (see photocopiable page 60). Put children in small groups or pairs, and provide a range of musical instruments and noise-making materials for them to experiment with. You could provide:
  - paper cups and plates for tapping, banging or rubbing together
  - paper of various kinds for crackling, tearing, flapping
  - corrugated paper and a pencil for a washboard effect
  - Brio cubes for banging together
  - metal, plastic or glass containers and a pencil for tapping and banging.

- Take the children through the story and give each group one sound effect to think about and represent. Let them demonstrate their efforts and talk about the sounds very explicitly, for example:
  - *That's a very mysterious sound – I love the high pitch and the way it wails up and down.*
  - *That's a great sound for water – I can imagine ripples lapping at the side of the lake.*

- Practise a 'production' of the story with children's voices and sound effects. You can vary the use of voices too, as appropriate to sections of the story:
  - choral recitation by the whole group
  - individual children's voices
  - paired or group voices (for example, all the girls or all the boys).

- Stage your production for other classes or parents, or record it on tape for the children to listen to.

You Can... Use storytime to develop mental imaging

Throughout history, listening to stories has helped children 'make pictures in their heads'. Don't let today's beautiful picture books prevent them from developing their own imaginative responses.

Thinking points

- As time moves on, you will move away from RA-RA-RA books, but some children with listening difficulties will still need regular opportunities for listening to and imitating short, repetitive texts. Make sure they get RA-RA-RA activities in small groups (not just practice of literacy subskills), perhaps sharing picture books with a teaching assistant or parent helper.
- It's also important to keep reading aloud, at an appropriate level, to the whole class every day – even when most of the children are able to read for themselves. As Robert Louis Stevenson said, we should always read to children, for how else will they learn 'the chime of fair words, and the march of the stately period?'

Tips, ideas and activities

- Listening to you tell stories is an obvious opportunity for children to develop visualisation skills. So although you may sometimes use puppets, pictures and objects to enhance your performance, don't always provide visual props. A simple story-map – using stick-men and symbols rather than proper pictures – leaves room for the imagination.

- Encourage visualisation sometimes when reading a picture book or in RA-RA-RA sessions (see page 40). Try covering up all the pictures with coloured paper. Introduce this activity by telling the children that you are not going to show them any pictures with this story – you want them to make their own in their heads.

- The first time you do this, give children paper and crayons and let them draw pictures to represent the story when they have listened to it. If you read the story daily as a Book of the Week, they could embellish these pictures each day, as they listen and join in. Perhaps at the end of the week, you could unveil the pictures in the book to compare with the children's own.

- Another time, choose a story that is easy to mime or dramatise, and tell children that when they have heard it, they are going to work in a group to act out the story. Provide puppets and a prop-box for them to act it out in 'free choice time' too.

- When you think the children have sufficient listening stamina, try reading a no-pictures story just for listening. Talk to children about the pictures it conjures up for them – colours, shapes, landscapes, people's expressions and clothes, etc.

- As children grow older and develop listening stamina, you can move from picture books to longer stories and 'chapter books' during storytime. These texts are too long for RA-RA-RA, but earlier RA-RA-RA activities should have prepared children to listen, concentrate and make their own pictures as you read.

You Can... Use storytime for listen–imitate–innovate activities

Both RA-RA-RA and oral storytelling involve listening and imitating. When children have internalised the language patterns, you can encourage them to innovate on them.

Thinking points

- There are a limited number of story structures in the world. Listen–imitate–innovate activities show children how to pick up and internalise basic story frameworks and make them their own. The underpinning structures by which people tell stories are language patterns. Children must internalise these through listening before they can successfully innovate on them and come up with successful stories of their own.

- In the early days of the National Literacy Strategy, we urged teachers to help children 'to read like a writer', picking up story structures, ideas and phrases they could use in their own work. Over time, however, it became clear that ,first, one has to 'listen like a prospective writer'. The ability to write fluently and easily depends upon:
    - mastery of the basic skills of handwriting and spelling
    - a deeply ingrained awareness of the patterns and rhythms of written language, born of effective listening.

Tips, ideas and activities

- Choose a familiar RA-RA-RA book and show it to the children. Then suggest making up your own story based on it. For instance, show *Owl Babies* by Martin Waddell (Walker) and say: *Let's not have three little owls today, let's have three something else...We could have monsters, lions, caterpillars...* Let the children choose, then put the book aside and start telling the story from memory, with the new characters. Adjust it as necessary as you go along, for example: *They lived in... where would they live?* Go back to the beginning each time and tell the story with the innovated characters, setting and events. When you have finished, children might like to draw or paint the new story.

- Use the same method with oral stories the children know well. Tell the story, with the actions, in the usual way, changing characters, setting and events. You could use the same basic story frame on several days, trying different innovations. Each time, of course, you will be revising the key language structures and connectives. There are plenty of suggestions and ideas in Pie Corbett's *Bumper Book* (see page 41).

You Can... Integrate listening into classroom routines

Classroom routines create a sense of security for young children and their regular repetition makes them ideal vehicles for listening skills. Routines requiring children to listen can be particularly helpful for those who find attention skills difficult.

Thinking points

- Routine and ritual are important for children because they help create secure neural networks into which other learning can be integrated. So children from homes where there is not a great deal of routine and stability benefit especially from daily rituals such as those above. If these are linked to listening skills, it should help them settle into the listening ethos of school education.

Tips, ideas and activities

- Two good ways to start the day are:
  - greeting children individually as they self-register and settle into the classroom, thus modelling social listening and encouraging children's talk
  - a 'Song and Rhyme Time', which helps tune children's brains to pattern and ears to sound before classwork begins. Singing and chanting together also involves working in harmony with others, a good socialising start to the day.

- Ensure you have storytime sessions at regular times each day – immediately after a break is a good time, because it gives a motivating reason to come in and settle back into class activities.

- Use songs and chants to signal changeover times during the day. Instead of calling children to attention, train them up to join in when they hear you start a particular song or chant. As they join in, they begin the relevant activity, for example:
  - made-up songs, like this one for 'Tidy Up Time':
    It's time to tidy up, it's time to tidy up,
    Ee aye addio, it's time to tidy up.
    We're clearing up the mess... etc
    We're putting stuff away...etc
    We're putting up the chairs... etc

- When children need to move around the school, for assembly, gym, etc, encourage them to march in time to a rhythm (and sing, as long as it doesn't disturb others).

- Use eye-contact (and silence!) as a 'choosing' strategy, for example: *I'm not going to say your name when it's time to get your coat today – I'm going to* look *at you.* When children have got the hang of this, invite one of them to do the eye contact: *Joanna is going to be the looker today. When she looks at you, go and get your coat.*

You Can... Use signs and symbols to save airspace

If we want children to listen to us, we have to be careful how we use our voices – putting some information into the visual field frees up the airspace for more important information.

Thinking points

- While repetition is of the essence in terms of children's learning, it is their repetition that counts, not yours. If you repeatedly explain aspects of class organisation or nag children about aspects of behaviour, they will learn to switch off, because this is not the sort of thing that motivates them. You want them to associate your voice with interesting, relevant listening experiences, not miserable ones.
- Contemporary children, brought up in a multimedia society, tend to find visual cues easy to remember, so they are a very helpful aid to classroom management.

Tips, ideas and activities

- Keep your voice for the listening activities that matter. Use visual alternatives to cover more workaday aspects of classroom life, such as organisation and behaviour management, for example:
  - use actions like holding up both hands and wiggling fingers (*Show me ten*) to tell children that silence is required – as they see you, they mimic your movements and fall silent
  - hold up or point to pictures, signs and symbols to remind children of behavioural rules, rather than repeatedly explaining or nagging.

- Make a visual timetable (see illustration) to show the events of the school day. Each day, attach cards with pictures/symbols in L>R sequence to indicate the events children can expect during that section of the day. Cue cards on photocopiable page 61 include activity symbols (going out to play, putting on coats, storytime, PE and changing for PE) and behaviour management cards (sit down, be quiet, look at the teacher and put up your hand). Encourage the children to keep an eye on the timetable so they are mentally prepared for each event. Boys particularly find it reassuring to know what is coming next.

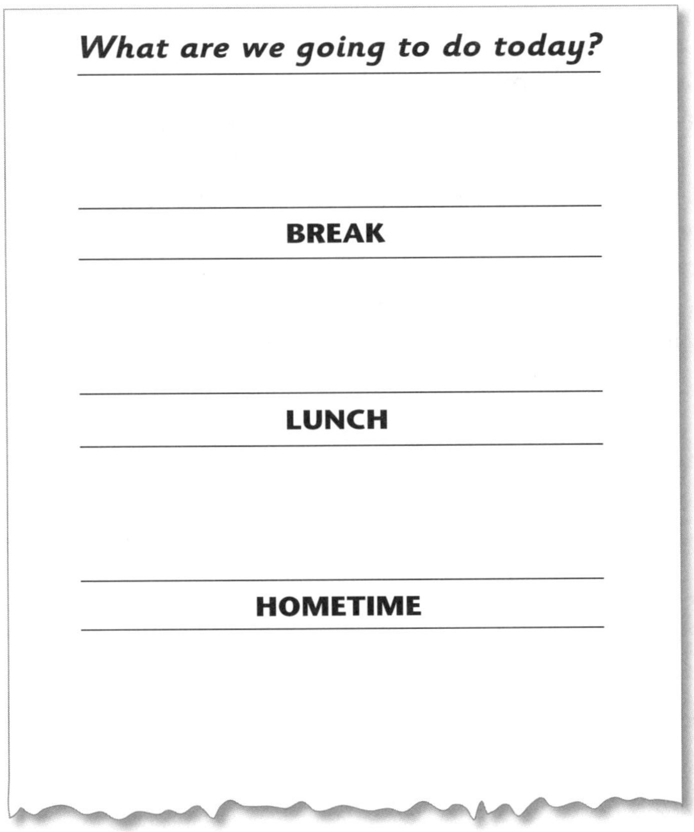

What are we going to do today?

BREAK

LUNCH

HOMETIME

- Use symbols for behaviour management, for example:
  - pictures or coloured cards you can carry with you, like a football referee, and show to rule-breakers (when someone is not attending, catch his eye by waving the 'Look at the teacher' card)
  - a puppet or soft toy who signals distress at particular behaviour (*Oh, I think Lola's upset about something. What do you think it is?*). Ros Bayley's *How to help Young Children to Listen* (Lawrence Education) provides many good ideas in this respect.

You Can... Create indoor listening areas

To ensure that children value listening and engage in it voluntarily during the school day, we need to provide appropriate environments.

Thinking points

- The success of indoor listening activities depends upon children being able to hear what is going on. Listening areas should therefore be in the quietest part of the classroom – or perhaps in nooks and crannies outside the main classroom area. But it is also important to keep classroom noise down at all times (see page 50).

Tips, ideas and activities

- Create cosy listening corners around the classroom where two or three children can go to talk and listen to each other during 'Free Time', for example:
  - use old curtains to create a Listening Tent
  - use furniture, card and fabric to make Listening Dens or Listening Caves.

Provide 'conversation boxes' in each, and every day put an interesting object or picture in the box for children to find and talk about. However, once the areas are established, they will probably use them to discuss their own topics and interests.

- Ensure that the listening corners are in areas shielded as far as possible from classroom noise. Make sure also that the seating in them is appropriate – many children need a hard surface to lean against in order to balance and sit still.

- Model how to use the listening corners, and discuss with children how they can best use them, and what behaviour is and isn't allowed.

- If there is enough space, provide a larger area for a regular Listening Table, which children can choose to visit during 'Free Time'. Here you could provide regular listening activities such as:
  - a listening centre with headphones for listening to stories
  - a tape recorder with commercial or home-made listening games
  - an adult who supervises a specific listening activity.

At this table, provide small chairs for the children, so they can sit comfortably and concentrate on listening.

You Can... Create outdoor listening areas

Outdoor listening areas provide opportunities to widen children's listening and learning, by alerting them to the natural world.

Thinking points

- Den-making is a natural impulse in young human beings, springing from the need to be safe in a dangerous world. Children instinctively want to go behind, under and inside overgrown areas, and to find quiet sanctuaries. Unfortunately, teachers tend to get anxious when children burrow off into the undergrowth (*What are you doing in there? Come out where I can see you!*), so today's young don't learn naturally to spend time in these quiet places. In the past, many children experienced some of this natural quiet in their beds at night, but with the advent of bedtime TV, quietness has been all but eradicated from their lives. We have to find ways of putting it back.
- The organisation, Learning Through Landscapes (www.ltl.org.uk) gives advice on the design of outdoor areas to provide both active play space and areas for quiet conversation and contemplation.

Tips, ideas and activities

- As well as providing plenty of active play areas outdoors (where children can be as noisy as they like, while letting off steam), set aside some quiet areas, in corners of your school grounds, for example:
  - an enclosed area big enough for outdoor circle time, where you can introduce the pleasure of listening to nature, as well as outdoor group speaking and listening activities
  - small, secluded corners for paired or small group conversations.

- If you are fortunate enough to have an outdoor wild area, let children create dens and caves, where they can go to listen to each other but also to enjoy the quietness of an enclosed space. You don't need to leave 'conversation boxes' in outdoor listening areas as children usually find their own objects to discuss.

- Make sure there are plenty of intimate seating areas – spaces with enough room for two or three children to sit and chat together. These don't need to be specially-made benches – logs, blocks or a section of wall will do just as well. But try to find ways of separating them from the hustle and bustle of other children's active play.

- Introduce children, through circle time or listening walks, to the pleasure of listening to the outside world – especially birdsong, the sounds of the weather and other natural sounds – and talking about what they hear with their friends. Model this with individuals and pairs by sitting with them in outdoor listening areas and drawing their attention to the sounds around them.

- Model also how to use outdoor listening areas for quiet conversations. All of these activities could take place during outdoor breaks or as 'Free Time' choices.

You Can... Keep noise levels down so children can listen

Children can't learn to listen in a noisy environment. It is up to the teacher to create a calm, quiet, purposeful ethos in the classroom so that listening is possible and enjoyable.

Thinking points

- It is staggeringly obvious that if we want children to learn to listen, they need a calm, quiet environment. But I know of a nursery where loud music is played all day long 'to stimulate the children' and have visited many Foundation and Key Stage 1 classes where noise levels were deafening. We value listening so little in our society that many teachers and practitioners simply don't think about it. They interpret 'child-centred' or 'play-based' activities as meaning that children should just do whatever they fancy, and – if children know no better – this often translates into simply running riot and making a great deal of noise. One of the main aims of early years education is to socialise children gradually and help them learn how to co-exist and work together in a small enclosed space. So running riot and making a lot of unnecessary noise indoors is not an option.

Tips, ideas and activities

- Start as you mean to go on. Make calm, quiet, purposeful activity your aim from day one. If you inherit a rowdy class, use:
  - games like those on pages 20–21 to develop children's self-control
  - songs, rhymes and storytime to focus their listening
  - circle time and classroom routines to develop social listening skills.

- Explain to the children that you run a calm classroom and, with older children, discuss how they can help you – if they have ownership of the rules and routines, they are more likely to follow them. Help them recognise the levels of noise that are acceptable – such as a low buzz of conversation 'in quiet indoor voices' – and congratulate children for appropriate behaviour, while clamping down immediately on loud shrieks, banging, etc. However, always model calm, quiet, purposeful behaviour yourself (let signs and symbols do your shouting for you).

- Make sure there is somewhere children *can* make a noise – boys especially need to be able to escape from your calm haven sometimes. Constant access to an outdoor area is ideal, especially if some of it is shielded from the classroom so noise doesn't penetrate. Provide lots of opportunities throughout the day for boisterous children to go out, run off energy and get noise out of their system. If there is no escape, it will be difficult for them to keep buttoned up indoors.

- As your class gradually become calm and quiet, congratulate them immoderately. Let them know that there are few other classes in the world that could achieve such grown-up, clever behaviour. You, their teacher, are blessed.

- There are more valuable suggestions in *You Can Create a Calm Classroom, 4–7* by Sue Cowley (Scholastic).

You Can... Develop social listening skills in collaborative group work

Once children are able to listen, we have to provide opportunities for them to listen to each other.

Thinking points

- Children who can't listen during large group or class activities are unlikely to benefit greatly from *unsupervised,* structured group work. What is more, their behaviour may well prevent other children from benefiting too. They first need to learn the skills of listening through the sorts of activities described throughout this book, including supervised group and classwork such as circle time. You can ensure inclusivity by involving them in the same activities as other children (where appropriate) with adult help.

Tips, ideas and activities

- Provide plenty of opportunities for:
  - unstructured, loosely supervised play, in which children can develop social listening skills naturally through their own self-chosen interactions
  - 'Free Time' self-chosen activities in which children can work individually, alongside each other, with opportunities for natural social interaction, leading to self-motivated communication.

Accept that these natural opportunities for speaking and listening cannot (and should not) be directed by you. Control of events must be in the hands of the children and – apart from intervention for reasons of safety or noise-abatement – they will gain far more if adults leave them to it.

- Once you feel children have learned basic listening skills (including active social listening), you can introduce independent structured group work, in which they can practise their speaking and listening skills with each other. For instance:
  - the sort of structured learning described on page 12, in which you introduce new vocabulary and concepts, and then provide group activities with opportunities for children to use new words and knowledge in context
  - drama or role-play activities in which children work as a group to devise and polish a short performance for the rest of the class
  - for children with reasonable reading skills, 'Readers' Theatre' activities, in which they take a short, familiar text and devise a presentation of it, using a variety of voices, voice combinations and sound effects.

- For children who are unable to work collaboratively in this way, use assessment procedures (see page 55 and photocopiable page 62) to decide which aspects of listening to target specifically – in an incremental way – to build up their skills. Give them plenty of opportunities to work in supervised groups (the more difficulties they have, the smaller the group) where they can try the same sort of activities as other children, but with adult support.

You Can... Organise paired speaking and listening

The Talking Partners technique – which provides excellent opportunities for developing both speaking and listening skills – is now widely used in primary schools, and can be highly effective with younger children as long as they are well trained in how to make the most of it.

Thinking points

- Asking children to talk and listen to each other is a great way of avoiding the 'I talk, they listen' trap. It gives every child the opportunity to speak and be heard. Across the curriculum, children always learn better when they have the chance to articulate their understanding.Specific talking points could include:
  - favourite foods, games, animals, TV programmes
  - things they like doing, places they like to visit
  - a time when they were excited or scared
  - a description of someone in their family
  - their favourite place at home
  - how they get home from school
  - things they think they are good at or find difficult
  - some work they have done in school
  - what they would choose if they could have any present they wanted.

Tips, ideas and activities

- When you think most children are ready, introduce Talking Partners during circle time (*Turn to the person on your left and say Hello...*). Give lots of experience in this type of structured setting for children to learn how to talk one-to-one with a peer. You could ask children, on different occasions, to talk about the topics in the box opposite:

- Use a sign or symbol to call the group back to order when you think they have had sufficient time – and, of course, build up their paired listening stamina gradually.

- Once the activity is familiar, add another dimension: *Today turn to the person on your left and name yourselves A and B. Now A is going to tell B about… B has to listen very carefully and then tell A what she/he thinks she/he said. A has to listen very carefully and help B get it right.* You could ask some of the Bs to re-tell their partner's contribution to the whole group. When they have got the idea, swap over and let B tell A, etc.

- Talk to children about what makes the Talking Partner technique work best – draw up a list of your class's rules for good paired speaking and listening.

- Once children are able to use the strategy, integrate it into the daily work of the class. For instance, children could turn to a Talking Partner:
  - during story-telling, and recite the story to each other, mirroring actions
  - while talking about picture books (*Tell your partner your ideas… about this character…what will happen next… etc*)
  - in class discussions (*Talk to your partner about the rules we need for…*).

- For children who find paired talk difficult, provide an adult partner (yourself, a teaching assistant, etc). If there are not enough adults to go round, work with them in a very small group. But if there are too many children who can't participate, concentrate on general listening skills before using the technique on a regular basis.

You Can... Develop listening in literacy and numeracy lessons

Once children's listening, language, attention and social skills are developed (usually by the age of 6+), they should be ready to learn the formal skills of reading, writing and number work.

Thinking points

- In most European countries, formal lessons in the 3Rs don't begin until children are six or seven years old, and the social and linguistic foundations of learning are well and truly laid. This is not to say that children who are ready to read, write or count are held back – informal opportunities for these activities are provided and children are supported and encouraged as individuals. The class focus, however, right up to the age of six or seven, is on oral learning, including the underlying concepts of literacy and numeracy. Watching this practice has convinced me that, while dictation and mental maths are appropriate for children at the top of Key Stage 1, before that they are less useful than oral activities. For ways of applying a European approach to literacy learning which is consistent with the requirements of the Foundation Stage Early Learning Goals, see *Foundations of Literacy* by Sue Palmer and Ros Bayley (Network Continuum).

Tips, ideas and activities

- In the early stages of phonics teaching, all activities should be oral, as the point is to develop recognition of the phonemes. However, when children have adequate phonic knowledge and pencil control (and not before!), use small handheld whiteboards for simple dictation practice. As always, tackle this incrementally, and don't move on until you are sure they are ready to succeed at the next stage:
  - start by asking children to listen and write single sounds
  - progress to CVC words
  - try some key 'sight' words that can't be decoded
  - move to short, simple sentences (such as *The cat sat on the mat*), which gives you an opportunity to highlight punctuation as well.

- With more able children of 7+, you should be able to progress to longer dictations on paper (perhaps two or three short sentences), featuring words they know well. Always
  - read the whole sentence through first
  - then read it in short grammatical chunks, giving time for writing
  - then read it through again for checking.

This activity develops focused listening, auditory memory, recognition of written language patterns and listening stamina.

- Number activities in the early stages should also be oral. As well as counting, activities such as those described on page 10 help children internalise number concepts.

- When children understand the number system and have sufficient hand control to write the numbers (and not before!), short mental maths sessions provide the same listening benefits as dictation. A useful resource for oral maths is *Maths Call* (Harper Collins). (NB Children with poor imaging skills find mental maths difficult – see pages 10, 24, 28, 37 and 44.)

You Can... Use ICT for focused listening

Too great a reliance on screen-based entertainment/education at an early age is more likely to inhibit listening skills than promote them. Young children need first-hand experiences and genuine human interaction. Teachers should ensure that any use of ICT is productive and encourages focused listening.

Thinking points

- On the whole, the message from neuroscience and developmental psychology is that, the younger the child, the more they need real-life, first-hand experience. For satisfactory cognitive development, much of that experience must be mediated by talk, both with caring adults and with peers. And to appreciate that talk, children need to be able to listen.

Tips, ideas and activities

- There are many ways in which ICT can be used to develop focused listening:
  - CD and cassette players can provide musical accompaniment and introduce new songs (but once the words and tunes are familiar, adults' sing-along models are required – see page 38)
  - listening games, such as sound identification games and 'Sound Bingo', on tape
  - 'talking stories' for a group of children to listen to through headphones on a 'listening centre'
  - TV, video and DVD for demonstrations of language for role-play (page 23) and clapping and other rhymes for rhythmic movement (page 31).

But when using such resources, do keep in mind your specific teaching objective and the underlying listening skills involved. Beware of resources that promise listening skills, but merely keep children entertained and/or occupied with fairly pointless tasks.

- Look out for further devices that could be helpful in developing the skills we have discussed, for example:
  - mini-recording devices that allow children to record sounds or their own voices
  - amplifiers for use in group or classwork, such as karaoke machines or mini-microphones (some teachers use these as the 'special object' passed around to signify whose turn it is during circle time – and the child can talk into the mike)
  - internet resources, such as the CBeebies website, where there are often listening games (but see these as a fun extension of your real-life listening activities, not as any sort of substitute).

- Make use of ICT for developing your own resources. For instance, when about to start work on a particular subject area, use a search engine to browse for songs, rhymes and stories. Three useful websites are:
  - www.bbc.co.uk/cbeebies
  - www.smart-central.com
  - www.bigeyedowl.co.uk

You Can... Assess listening skills without making a meal of it

Fortunately, the government has not yet devised formal tests and targets for listening skills, so teachers are free to assess their children's development in sensible, useful, non-time-consuming ways.

Thinking points

Analysing the assessment sheet:

(a)s and (b)s across the board may simply mean the child has not developed listening skills naturally (in which case, you can hope for steady progress using the activities described here). But if there are a great many (a)s, or if the child does not make progress, refer to a speech and language therapist for assessment.

In the following more specific scenarios, difficulties could again simply be due to poor listening skills, so try the appropriate activities. But if the child does not make progress and is still scoring:

- (a)s and (b)s specifically on 1 and 2, it could indicate dyspraxia – check with the Senco to be on the safe side.
- (a)s and (b)s on question 2 onwards, she/he could have hearing problems (either general or intermittent hearing loss) – check with parents and/or refer to the school doctor or audiometrician.
- (a)s on questions 3, 4, 5 and 6, she/he could be on the autistic spectrum – check with the Senco.
- (a)s on questions 4, 5 and 6, she/he could have emotional difficulties – perhaps arrange a meeting with parents and the Senco.
- (a)s and (b)s specifically on questions 7 and 8, this could be an indicator of dyslexia – check with the Senco.

Tips, ideas and activities

- If children's listening seems to be developing satisfactorily, don't bother with formal assessment. You will be able to spot that children have:
  - physical control and balance (through their ability to stand/sit still when required)
  - discriminative listening skills (through their performance in games)
  - social listening skills (in their general social interaction and behaviour in circle time)
  - good auditory memory (by their ability to memorise songs, rhymes and stories)
  - listening stamina (by their tolerance of listening activities).

- If a child is giving no cause for concern, just keep on with focused incremental teaching until you no longer need to teach listening skills, but can use children's established skills to underpin learning across the curriculum.

- During everyday activities, concentrate your attention on those children who are having difficulties. Use the rule-of-thumb checklist on photocopiable page 62 to get an indication of where problems might lie (see box), and provide more incremental practice of the skills that seem to be giving them trouble. But if you are in any doubt, always refer children on to the relevant expert. As the box shows, in a small proportion of cases, an inability to listen may be the result of a physical or developmental disorder.

- As for children's phonemic awareness, keep an eye on the list on page 56 and, where a child seems to be having trouble with a particular sound, give plenty of practice of an appropriate rhyme. However, if you have any serious cause for concern, contact a speech and language therapist for an assessment.

The phonemes of English

Consonant phonemes with consistent spellings

/b/	**b**at, ra**bb**it
/d/	**d**og, da**dd**y
/g/	**g**irl, gi**gg**le
/h/	**h**ot
/l/	**l**og, lo**ll**y
/m/	**m**at, su**mm**er
/n/	**n**ut, di**nn**er
/p/	**p**ig, su**pp**er
/r/	**r**at, ca**rr**y
/t/	**t**op, pa**tt**er
/y/	**y**ellow
/th/	**th**is (voiced) **th**ing (unvoiced)

Consonant phonemes with alternative spellings

/k/	**c**at, **k**ing, ba**ck,** s**ch**ool, **q**ueen (also the /k/ sound in bo**x**)
/s/	**s**un, pre**ss**, **c**ircle
/f/	**f**un, **ph**oto
/j/	**j**am, **g**inger, bri**dge**
/w/	**w**orm, q**u**een
/z/	**z**oo, pin**s**, **x**ylophone
/v/	**v**an (one exception: o**f**)
/sh/	**sh**eep, sta**ti**on, **ch**ef
/ch/	**ch**in, i**tch**
/ng/	si**ng**, pi**n**k
/zh/	mea**s**ure, a**z**ure

Age at which children usually pronounce the consonant phonemes

'Short' and 'long' vowel phonemes

/a/	b**a**g
/e/	b**e**t, br**ea**d, s**ai**d
/i/	b**i**g, c**y**linder
/o/	t**o**p, w**a**s
/u/	b**u**n, l**o**ve
/ae/	d**ay**, p**ai**n, g**a**t**e**, gr**ea**t
/ee/	f**ee**t, s**ea**t, P**e**t**e**, m**e**
/ie/	t**ie**, t**igh**t, fl**y**, t**i**m**e**
/oa/	b**oa**t, gr**ow**, b**o**n**e**, t**oe**, g**o**
/ue/	bl**ue**, m**oo**n, gr**ew**, fl**u**t**e**, y**ou**

Other vowel phonemes

/oo/	g**oo**d, p**u**t, c**oul**d, w**o**lf
/ur/	ch**ur**ch, b**ir**d, h**er**b, **ear**th, w**or**d
/ar/	st**ar**t, f**a**ther
/or/	c**or**n, d**oor**, sh**ore**, r**oar**, y**our**
/aw/	p**aw**, t**au**t, t**a**ll, t**a**lk, t**augh**t
/ow/	cl**ow**n, sh**ou**t
/oy/	b**oy**, **oi**l
/ear/	n**ear**, d**eer**, h**ere**
/air/	ch**air**, sh**are**, th**ere**
/oor/	p**oor**, s**ure**

There is also the 'schwa' (a sort of indeterminate grunting sound) as in farm**er**, doct**or**, gramm**ar**, metr**e**, col**our**, Americ**a**...

Recommended poems and rhymes

Julius Caesar
Julius Caesar, the Roman geezer,
Squashed his wife in a lemon squeezer.

Caterpillar
Brown and furry
Caterpillar in a hurry,
Take your walk
To the shady leaf or stalk
Or what not,
Which may be the chosen spot.
No toad spy you,
Hovering bird of prey pass by you;
Spin and die...
To live again, a butterfly.
Christina Rossetti

Nobody Likes Me
Nobody likes me,
Everybody hates me,
Going outside to eat worms.

Big fat squishy ones,
Short thin skinny ones,
See how they squiggle and squirm.

Bite off their heads,
And suck the juices,
And throw their skins away.
Nobody knows how much I thrive,
On worms three times a day.

I Hear Thunder
I hear thunder
I hear thunder
Hark, don't you?
Hark don't you?
Pitter patter raindrops
Pitter patter raindrops
I'm wet through
So are you.

The Bear Went over the Mountain
(sung to the tune of 'For He's a Jolly Good Fellow')
The bear went over the mountain, the bear went over the mountain,
The bear went over the mountain, to see what he could see.
And all that he could see, and all that he could see,
Was the other side of the mountain, the other side of the mountain, was all that he could see.

So he went back over the mountain, he went back over the mountain,
He went back over the mountain, to see what he could see.
And all that he could see, and all that he could see,
Was the other side of the mountain, the other side of the mountain, was all that he could see.

So... (Repeat second verse... forever!)

Letter to parents 1

Dear Parent or Carer,

Song and Rhyme Time

Every week throughout this year, your child will bring home a short song or rhyme to learn by heart. We would be very grateful if you could help with this, by singing or chanting along with your child until she/he knows it.

Just before bedtime and first thing in the morning are good times to practise. And as your child builds up a repertoire, could you have a 'Song and Rhyme Time' session every so often and revise the lot (perhaps in the car, or to fill in time at a bus stop)?

The rhymes and songs don't take long to learn because they're quite short, but it could help your child's education a great deal. They are an enjoyable way of developing an essential learning skill known as auditory memory. In the past, most children developed their auditory memory fairly naturally but, in today's multimedia world, this often doesn't happen.

The better their auditory memory, the easier children find it to spell words correctly, remember facts, solve maths problems and do many other basic educational tasks.
Thank you very much for your help.

Yours sincerely,

Class Teacher

Letter to parents 2

Dear Parent or Carer,

Read aloud, read along, read alone

Your child is bringing home a RA-RA-RA book. This is short for 'Read Aloud, Read Along, Read Alone'. We hope you'll be able to share many favourite RA-RA-RA books in the coming months.

We have chosen these books because they're great fun to share with children and, if you read them aloud a few times, your child will start joining in ('reading along') with you. Soon, she/he may be able to 'read' the book alone.

To begin with, of course, this is not real reading – just reciting from memory. But, as I said in a previous letter, auditory memory is an extremely important skill. Also, children who have fun sharing books in this way are more likely to be keen readers in the future.

When – later in the year – your child learns how to match sounds (like **c-a-t**) to words ('cat!'), we'll help make the link between 'reading' the RA-RA-RA books and alphabet decoding.

In the meantime, we hope you can spare the time to share this book – and others – with your child, and give plenty of praise when she/he joins in (and perhaps 'takes over') the reading. Thank you very much for your help.

Yours sincerely,

Class Teacher

Some tried and tested RA-RA-RA books

Alfie Gets in First by Shirley Hughes (Red Fox)
Angry Arthur by Hiawyn Oram and Satsoshi Kitamura (Red Fox)
The Animal Boogie by Debbie Harter (Barefoot Paperback)
Bearobics by Emily Bolam and Vic Parker (Hodder Children's Books)
The Bear Under the Stairs by Helen Cooper (Corgi)
Billy's Sunflower by Nicola Moon (Little Hippo)
Brown Bear, Brown Bear, What Do You See? by Bill Martin jr and Eric Carle (Puffin)
Commotion in the Ocean by Giles Andreae (Ted Smart)
Danny's Duck by June Crebbin (Walker Books)
Dear Zoo by Rod Campbell (Puffin)
Doctor Dog by Babette Cole (Red Fox)
Dogger by Shirley Hughes (Picture Lions)
Duck in the Truck by Jez Alborough (Collins)
Each Peach Pear Plum by Janet and Allan Ahlberg (Puffin)
The Elephant and the Bad Baby by Elfrida Vipont and Raymond Briggs (Puffin)
Elmer by David McKee (Red Fox)
Farmer Duck by Martin Waddell (Walker)
The Fish who could Wish by John Bush and Korky Paul (Oxford University Press)
Five Little Ducks by Ian Beck (Orchard)
Funnybones by Janet and Allan Ahlberg (Puffin)
The Gingerbread Boy by Ian Beck (Oxford University Press)
Giraffes Can't Dance by Giles Andreae and Guy Parker-Rees (Ted Smart)
Hairy Maclary from Donaldson's Dairy by Lynley Dodd (Puffin)
Handa's Surprise by Eileen Browne (Walker)
Hector's New Trainers by Amanda Vesey (Picture Lions)
If You Want to be a Cat by Joyce Dunbar and Allan Curless (Macdonald Young Books)
It was Jake by Anita Jeram (Walker Books)
Jamaica and Brianna by Juanita Havill (Mammoth)
The Lion who Wanted to Love by Giles Andreae and David Wojtowycz (Orchard Books)
Little Rabbit Foo Foo by Michael Rosen and Arthur Robbins (Walker)
Mr Gumpy's Outing by John Burningham (Red Fox)
Mr Magnolia by Quentin Blake (Red Fox)
My Cat Likes to Hide in Boxes by Eve Sutton and Lynley Dodd (Puffin)
Not Now Bernard by David McKee (Red Fox)
One Snowy Night by Nick Butterworth (Collins)
Over in the Meadow by Louise Voce (Walker Books)
Owl Babies by Martin Waddell (Walker)
Pants by Nick Sharratt (Orchard)
Pass it, Polly by Sarah Garland (Puffin)
Pass the Jam, Jim by Kaye Umansky and Margaret Chamberlain (Red Fox)
Peace at Last by Jill Murphy (Macmillan)
Pop Goes the Weasel (Macmillan Big Poetry Book)
Rosie's Walk by Pat Hutchinson (Red Fox)
Row Your Boat by Pippa Goodhart (Picture Mammoth)
Rumble in the Jungle by Giles Andreae and David Wojtowycz (Orchard Books)
Solo by Paul Geraghty (Hutchinson)
So Much by Trish Cooke (Walker Books)
Suddenly! by Colin McNaughton (Collins)
Tall Inside by Jean Richardson (Picture Puffins)
The Tiger who Came to Tea by Judith Kerr (Collins)
The Time it Took Tom by Nick Sharratt (Scholastic)
The Train Ride by June Crebbin and Stephen Lambert (Walker)
This is the Bear by Sarah Hayes and Helen Craig (Walker)
Through my Window by Tony Bradman and Eileen Browne (Mammoth)
Tortoise's Dream by Joanna Troughton (Puffin)
The Very Hungry Caterpillar by Eric Carle (Puffin)
We're Going on a Bear Hunt by Michael Rosen and Helen Oxenbury (Walker)
Where the Wild Things Are by Maurice Sendak (Red Fox)
Where's My Teddy? by Jez Alborough (Walker)
Where's Spot? by Eric Hill (Puffin)

Cue cards

Activity cards:

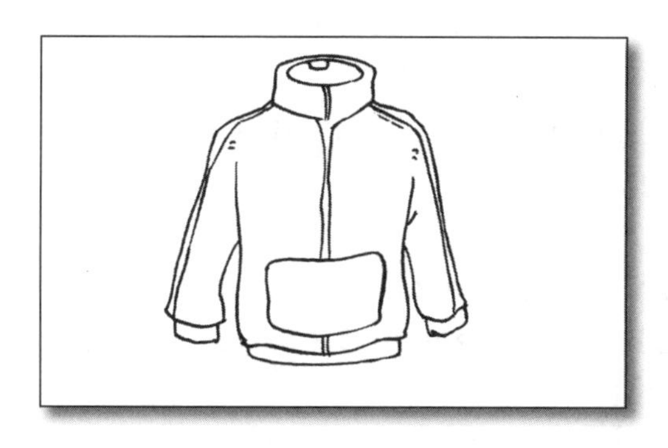

Behaviour management cards:

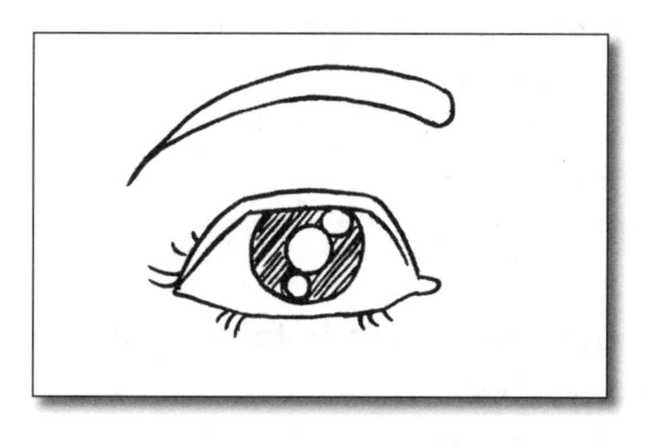

Listening assessment sheet

1. I am generally in control of my movements:

a) hardly any of the time
b) part of the time
c) most of the time
d) all of the time

2. I can:

a) not sit still at all
b) sit still for a short period when engaged in a task that interests me
c) sit still for extended periods when the task interests me
b) sit still when the teacher asks me to

3. I make eye contact:

a) when someone physically directs my face to the speaker
b) when I hear someone call my name
c) when someone is speaking directly to me
d) with the teacher when she is talking to the class

4. I can take my turn in conversations:

a) never
b) in directed one-to-one activities with an adult
c) in structured situations such as circle time
d) in general, during social interactions with others

5. When we play listening games, I:

a) don't follow the rules
b) can follow the rules as long as they suit me
c) take a long time to learn the rules
d) learn and follow rules quite quickly

6. In circle time:

a) I stay silent and/or look bewildered
b) I copy what others say, but rather hesitantly
c) I join in, sometimes copying, but sometimes making my own contributions
d) I join in confidently, and make innovative contributions

7. I find learning rhymes and songs:

a) very difficult and take a very long time to remember them, if ever
b) quite difficult and I muddle words, lose the rhythm, don't remember rhymes
c) reasonably easy as long as I get lots of repetition
d) pretty easy

8. When the class is joining in with stories:

a) I look uninterested or bewildered
b) I make movements with my mouth, but don't keep up
c) I join in and learn the words with plenty of repetition
d) I learn refrains and repeated words easily, and am soon word-perfect

Index

SCHOLASTIC

Also available in this series:

ISBN 978-0439-94532-5

ISBN 978-0439-94533-2

ISBN 978-0439-96522-4

ISBN 978-0439-96523-1

ISBN 978-0439-96534-7

ISBN 978-0439-96539-2

ISBN 978-0439-96540-8

ISBN 978-0439-96554-5

ISBN 978-0439-96555-2

ISBN 978-0439-94530-1

ISBN 978-0439-94531-8

ISBN 978-0439-94559-2

ISBN 978-0439-94554-7

To find out more, call: 0845 603 9091
or visit our website www.scholastic.co.uk